THE STORY OF THE

HITLER'S INFAMOUS LEGIONS OF DEATH

Many of the SS leadership, including Himmler and Heydrich, imagined they belonged to a line of Nordic knights from Germany's mythical past

stood by and watched them take place. Simply being a member of the SS was to be part of a huge criminal conspiracy. This was the banality of evil writ large.

'All my life I have wrestled with one question,' said Mauersberger. 'How could it be that a man from such a respectable home, with those humanist ideals, with those visions and aspirations, could end up in the SS?'

It cannot be said that the answer can only be found deep within the German psyche. When we look into the glass we are met with our own reflection. As well as German nationals, the ranks of the SS were swollen by French, Dutch, Belgian, Danish, Latvian, Ukrainian, Hungarian, Italian, Croatian and even Bosnian Muslim recruits. A number of Britons and Americans also joined, though they tended to be half-hearted in their approach. Most SS men did not appear to be at all discouraged by the losses they sustained and, when it became clear that Germany was going to lose the war, they went about their murderous activities all the more fanatically.

When the war was over, only a handful of SS murderers showed any remorse. Those who were executed often went to the gallows protesting the justness of their cause. Many did not pay such a high price, however. A

large number of war criminals had their death sentences commuted. After a relatively short period of imprisonment they were allowed to resume their daily lives in the normal world, a million miles away from their hideous crimes. Others fled to South America or the Middle East, where they continued to extol the virtues of National Socialism. Some even found safe havens in Britain, the United States and Canada, where they lived out their lives in comfort, without ever having to answer for their foul crimes.

The story of the SS has been told before, but it is well worth telling it again before the events fade from living memory. Hopefully we can all take heed of this warning from history. Germany is a country that has produced some of the greatest scientists, philosophers, musicians and artists the world has ever seen and yet it was able to experience a moment of terrifying madness. It could all happen again somewhere else if we do not remain vigilant. We must make sure that the seeds that blossomed as the stinking flower of the SS are not sown again. The people who joined the SS were not monsters or aliens but human beings who were not so very different from ourselves.

Nigel Cawthorne, Bloomsbury

CHAPTER ONE
The *Schutzstaffel*

Hitler was a complete nonentity until 1919, yet he ended up dominating the political landscape of the 20th century. A number of factors contributed to his meteoric rise to power, but a significant part of his success can be attributed to the physical intimidation of his opponents, and the German people, by the *Sturmabteilung* (SA) and the *Schutzstaffel* (SS).

The Treaty of Versailles (28 June 1919)

THE peace treaty that ended the First World War attributed all of the guilt to Germany alone. Germany was in no position to resume hostilities, so the nation's politicians were forced to accede to the harsh terms within the contract. For a start, it was ordered that reparations totalling 132 billion gold marks should be paid to the Allies. In addition, a number of European territories had to be surrendered. These were handed over to the newly re-established state of Poland and newly created Czechoslovakia. The Rhineland, lying between Germany and France, was demilitarized and the German army was reduced to 100,000 men. Germany would not be allowed to possess tanks, military planes or poison gas and the naval fleet could only retain a dozen battleships. All submarines were banned. On a more personal note, the Kaiser was declared a war criminal, together with a number of other Germans.

Germany was already heavily in debt after the war, so it could not pay the reparations. As a result, France and Belgium occupied the Ruhr, Germany's industrial heartland, in 1923. The German workers went on strike in the same year, but the government continued to pay them, thereby pushing the already devalued currency into a state of hyperinflation. For example, a loaf of bread that cost 20,000 marks in the morning cost 5 million marks by nightfall. The German state experienced complete economic collapse on 15 November 1923, when the exchange rate stood at over four trillion marks to $1. A lifetime's savings would not even buy a ticket for the U-bahn (the rapid transit railway in Berlin).

Catastrophe was averted when the Allies ended the occupation of the Ruhr and granted Germany 800 million gold marks in loans. The situation was eased still further when reparations were cut by two-thirds and the payments were rescheduled. This was not good enough for press and movie baron Alfred Hugenberg, leader of the German National People's Party. He employed Hitler to lead a campaign against the settlement, in which he demanded the end of all reparations and the removal of the so-called guilt clause.

Röhm's SA was made up of former members of the *Freikorps*, which had been officially disbanded after its failed 1920 putsch. SA troops wore distinctive brown shirts, in emulation of the black shirts worn by the followers of Benito Mussolini, who came to power in Italy after the March on Rome (*see* box, p.22) in 1922. As well as 'keeping order' at Nazi Party meetings, the SA also used coshes and knuckledusters to disrupt the meetings of rival parties. On one occasion in 1922, Hitler himself stormed on to a rival's platform and physically assaulted the speaker. He was sentenced to three months' imprisonment.

Stosstrupp Adolf Hitler

From the very start Hitler realized that he was constantly in personal danger. He had upset too many people for things to be otherwise. At first he had looked to Röhm's SA for protection but by 1923 he began to see the SA as a threat. Röhm could call on the support of his brown-shirted thugs whenever they were needed, even against Hitler if he so desired. Unnerved by this thought, Hitler ordered the formation of a personal bodyguard, which would be commanded by two of his trusted comrades, Julius Schreck and Joseph Berchtold. At first it was called the *Stabswache* (Security

The *Stosstrupp-Hitler* in September 1923 shortly before the Munich Putsch; five men were killed in the uprising and the squad was disbanded

Guard), but it was quickly renamed *Stosstrupp Adolf Hitler* (Adolf Hitler Shock Troop).

As Hitler said:

Being convinced that there are always circumstances in which elite troops are called for, I created in 1922–3 the 'Adolf Hitler Shock Troop'. It was made up of men who were ready for revolution and knew that some day things would come to hard knocks.

Hitler described his *Stosstrupp* as 'the first group of toughs'. Its original members were:

Julius Schreck (1898–1936)
Veteran of the First World War and the *Freikorps*, he had helped form the *Stabswache*. As Hitler's bodyguard and chauffeur, he took part in the Beer Hall Putsch and was incarcerated with Hitler in Landsberg Prison. A founder member of the SS, he was given a state funeral.

Mercedes from the Berlin Motor Show. He was seen to be betraying 'socialism' to further his own ends. This was not what the Brownshirts were getting broken bones and cracked skulls for.

As the 1930 election approached, the leader of the SA in Berlin, Walter Stennes, supplied Hitler with a list of demands. If he wanted the SA to support him at the polls he would have to add SA men to the list of candidates to the Reichstag; provide the SA with the sole responsibility for security at Nazi Party meetings; and stop Nazi *Gauleiters* interfering in SA matters. This was a direct challenge to the SS and the SA wanted paying well for the privilege. Hitler refused even to discuss the matter and then he issued a list of prospective candidates that did not even include Stennes' name.

In retaliation, Stennes sent a troop of Brownshirts along to break up a meeting at the Palace of Sports, where Goebbels was giving a speech. Goebbels called on the SS for protection but two days later a mob of SA troops smashed up the Nazi Party headquarters in Berlin and attacked the SS men on guard. The affair ended with the arrest of 25 SA men. Hitler rushed to Berlin, apparently to make peace with Stennes, and he seemingly caved in to all of his demands. He then recalled Röhm from Bolivia and asked him to take over as head of the SA. While Röhm was not Hitler's greatest fan – 'Dolf is an ass' he wrote to a friend in 1928 – he still had a considerable following in the SA.

But even Röhm could not restrain Stennes, who accused Hitler and Goebbels of betraying the National Socialist ideal. At a secret meeting of SA commanders in Berlin, it was decided to take no further orders from Hitler. Then the SA took over the Party headquarters in Berlin, along with the offices of the Nazi newspaper *Der Angriff* (The Attack). The SS fought back

Walter Stennes was one of the few Nazis to fall out with Hitler and live to tell the tale: he went on to work for Chiang Kai-shek in China

but its troops were heavily outnumbered. Finally a leaflet was circulated, which carried the message that Goebbels had been deposed as *Gauleiter* of Berlin.

'The SA is on the march. Stennes is in command,' it said.

In response, the Nazi Party expelled any SA units that rebelled. This deprived the rebels of the funds that Hitler had brought in from the business corporations that backed him. Stennes' support melted away and in 1933 he left Germany to command Chiang Kai-shek's bodyguard in China.

Heydrich and the SD

Throughout the rebellion, the SS had remained loyal and Hitler now depended on the force to root out any further dissent. Himmler's obsession with record-keeping now came into its own and his records of suspect Party

Members of the SS elite at Wannsee, 1934: (front row) Daluege, Himmler, Milch, Krügel, Von Schütz; (back row) Wolff, Bonin, Heydrich

members were used to purge all those who opposed Hitler. Himmler was helped in this enterprise by a new recruit named Reinhard Heydrich.

Although Heydrich became Himmler's most-trusted henchman, Himmler was not at first interested in the would-be recruit, to the extent that he cancelled an appointment with him. Undeterred, Heydrich turned up anyway. When Himmler saw him he was impressed with his Nordic looks and his rabid anti-Semitism.

'I want to set up a security and information service within the SS and I need a specialist,' Himmler said. 'If you think you can do this management job, will you please write down on paper how you think you would tackle it? I will give you twenty minutes.'

Off the top of his head, Heydrich sketched out a plan for the *Sicherheitsdienst* (SD; Security

Service). He was instantly hired. Heydrich then moved into the Brown House, the Nazi Party's new headquarters in Munich. After being shown into a shared room with only one typewriter, he was put to work at a kitchen table. In spite of the conditions, he set up a system of index cards that held details of aristo-crats, communists, Catholics, conservatives, politically active Jews and Freemasons. He also kept a record of any Nazis who had been made unreliable by heavy debts or scandal of any kind. Jewish communists, socialists or Freema-sons went into a special 'poison' file.

According to one of Himmler's confidants, Heydrich's mind was a 'living card index, a brain with all the threads woven together'. After less than four months in the job Heydrich told a meeting of SS officers that the Party was riddled with spies and saboteurs. He recommended that every SS unit should create

The 9th Nuremberg Rally (1937) was named the 'Rally of Labour' to highlight the reduction in unemployment since the Nazis had come to power

Oberführer Hermann Behrends, was appointed as Lorenz's deputy, so that the VoMi could be used to investigate ethnic Germans who were not politically reliable in the eyes of the SS. The SS also took over such seemingly innocuous organizations as the German Bulgarian Society.

After attaining a doctorate in law at the University of Marburg, Behrends joined the Nazi Party and the SS in 1932. He became the first head of the SD in Berlin and he is thought to have been responsible for some of the death lists that were used on the Night of the Long Knives. In 1937 he joined the VoMi, where he built up lists of ethnic Germans who were not considered politically reliable abroad. He also joined the *Waffen-SS*.

Later on he became the Higher SS and police leader in Yugoslavia, where he was respon-

sible for a number of atrocities. In 1945 he was arrested by the British in Flensburg. Handed back to the Yugoslavs, he was executed in Belgrade in 1946.

Nazi foreign policy

Himmler soon had another opportunity to get involved in Nazi foreign policy. Following the reorganization of the army that had followed the allegations against Blomberg and Fritsch in 1938, Hitler also sacked his foreign minister, Konstantin von Neurath, a veteran who had been inherited from von Papen. Von Neurath was replaced with Himmler's man, Joachim von Ribbentrop. Himmler had been cultivating Ribbentrop since he first joined the Party in 1932 and he had made him an honorary SS colonel. Ribbentrop was a vain man who liked

The 10th Nuremberg Rally in 1938 was devoted to 'Greater Germany' after *Anschluss* with Austria. Hitler's forces were readying for war

to wear the black uniform of the SS, so he welcomed the opportunity to be a member of the foreign ministry staff, working with SS men.

After being educated in Germany, Switzerland, France and England, Ribbentrop was in Canada when the First World War broke out in 1914. Eager to serve his country, he returned to Germany and served as a hussar on the Eastern Front, before becoming an intelligence officer in Turkey. After the war, he married the daughter of a producer of *Sekt* – the German version

of champagne – and he persuaded a distant, noble relative to adopt him so he could add the prefix 'von' to his name. Then in 1932 he met Hitler and joined the Nazi Party, becoming Hitler's chief foreign policy adviser by the simple expedient, it is said, of memorizing Hitler's words and repeating them back to him. Between 1936 and 1938 he was the German ambassador to the Court of St James's, where his mission was to forge an alliance between Germany and the British Empire. Instead he

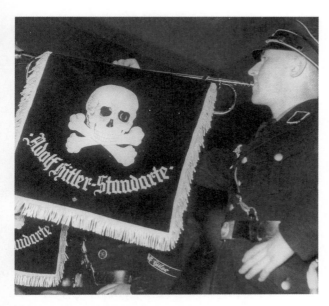

An 'asphalt soldier' with trumpet in 1933: at first SS men performed as ceremonial guards, waiters and musicians on state occasions

THE FIRST OFFICIALLY armed SS unit was the *Leibstandarte SS Adolf Hitler*. Formed in 1933, the force originally numbered just 100 men. Its troops were paid by the Prussian provincial police force and trained by the elite Ninth Regiment of the *Reichswehr*, the defence force of the Weimar Republic that became the *Wehrmacht* when conscription was reintroduced in 1935. At first, the *Leibstandarte* was dismissed as a unit of 'asphalt soldiers' – ceremonial guards who also acted as waiters and musicians on state occasions.

This was not good enough for Himmler. He wanted to turn the SS into a fully fledged military formation that would be completely under his control. In September 1934, he prevailed upon war minister Werner von Blomberg to allow him to set up an SS 'rapid-reaction force' known as the *SS-Verfügungstruppe* (Disposition Troops or SS-VT). This would have the strength of three regiments, along with an intelligence section.

Only months after the destruction of the SA in the Night of the Long Knives, the army had another rival.

Junkerschulen

While the *Wehrmacht* recruited its officers from among Prussian aristocrats – the Junkers – would-be SS officers were drawn from a broader social background. As a result, special officer training schools had to be set up for them, where they could learn the social graces as well as military tactics. These were called *Junkerschulen*, or schools for young noblemen. Candidates came from the SS, the SA and the Gestapo. They had to be recommended by their commanding officers and be over 5ft 10in (1.78m) tall.

The educational programme of the schools was extremely varied. Trainee officers were first of all given basic military training, which included playing war games on sand tables. They also studied *Mein Kampf* and were given lessons in etiquette – 'Cutlery is held only with the fingers and not with the whole hand'– and letters were to be ended with 'Heil Hitler, Yours sincerely…' There was an initial emphasis on racial purity, but this requirement had to be dropped during the war when recruits were accepted from the occupied countries. At that point, lectures on the sanctity of Nordic blood were replaced by talks on the evils of Bolshevism.

There was also a stress on physical fitness, which prepared the men for the mobile fighting that characterized the very end of the Second World War. The *SS-Junkerschule* at Bad Tölz was built with slave labour from Dachau. It had a soccer stadium surrounded by an athletics track, a heated swimming pool, a sauna and buildings dedicated to boxing, gymnastics and indoor ball games. At one time eight of

Physical fitness was a large part of the curriculum at *Junkerschule*:
Bad Tölz was built by slave labour and opened by Hitler in 1936

the twelve coaches were the German national champions in their fields. Duels using swords or pistols were also allowed. Himmler decreed that 'every SS man has the right and duty to defend his honour by force of arms'.

Military training was given by ex-*Reichswehr* men. Not everyone came up to scratch. Only one recruit in three made it to the end of the five-month course. Graduates were known for their bravery – or recklessness. Alumni of Bad Tölz suffered a fatality rate of 70 per cent on the battlefield.

A second *Junkerschule* at Brunswick was run by Paul Hausser, who became an inspector of the SS-VT with the rank of brigadier. Under his leadership the SS-VT was fashioned into an effective fighting force. In the autumn of 1937, Himmler was able to remark with pride: 'The *SS-Verfügungstruppe* is, according to the present standards of the *Wehrmacht*, prepared for war.'

However, the *Wehrmacht* still had a monopoly of heavy armaments. And through the *Wehrbezirkskommandos* (local recruitment offices or WBKs) the army could restrict the growth of the SS-VT by assigning it a relatively low quota of men. This ended with the reorganization of the army following the sacking of Fritsch and Blomberg. Hitler was now in control. On 17 August 1938 he decreed that the *Verfügungstruppe* was to be expanded to full divisional strength. It would then be used for 'special internal political tasks' and front-line fighting in the event of war.

Himmler's private army

Himmler now had his own private army. It comprised two SS regiments, *Deutschland* and *Germania*, a communications detachment and the *Leibstandarte*, which had already seen action in the march into the Ruhr in 1936 and now numbered 800 troops. A key figure was Felix

Graduates of Bad Tölz were known for their bravery, or recklessness, and suffered a fatality rate of 70 per cent

Steiner, commander of the Munich-based SS regiment *Deutschland*, who armed some of his men with machine guns and grenades, instead of rifles, for greater killing power. He also adopted the newly designed camouflage battle-dress and bred in his men a distinctive *esprit de corps*. Hausser complained that the *Deutschland* troops were Himmler's 'favourite babies'.

Unlike many of his peers, who used their positions to pursue their private fantasies, Steiner was a simple, straightforward career officer. He won the Iron Cross in the First World War and when the hostilities ended he led a unit of the *Freikorps*. In 1922, he rejoined the *Reichswehr*. When the Nazis came to power Steiner was involved in army training, when he became impressed by the methods used by the SS-VT. In 1935 he took command of a battalion of *SS-Verfügungstruppen* and was subsequently promoted to SS colonel before being given the command of the *SS-Deutschland* Regiment.

He led the regiment during the invasion of Poland and France, earning the Knight's Cross. Himmler then employed him to oversee the creation of the 5th SS Panzer Division *Wiking*, which was mainly composed of volunteers from the Netherlands, Belgium and Scandinavia. With the addition of a number of Latvian

Felix Steiner was a key figure in the *Deutschland* regiment. He armed his men with machine guns and grenades for greater killing power

volunteers, he formed the III (Germanic) SS Panzer Corps, which fought in Russia. Less bloodthirsty than many of his peers, Steiner refused to obey the order to summarily execute all of the Soviet commissars, though some of his *Wikings* are known to have committed documented massacres.

Despite his loyalty to Hitler, he also disobeyed the order to break the encirclement of Berlin. Instead, he saved his men from certain annihilation by moving west to avoid capture by the Soviets. Hitler had ceased to think or act rationally at this point, 22 April 1945, but he launched into a weak tirade all the same.

Steiner will not attack? Steiner is disobeying a direct order from your Führer, your Chancellor, and your Party head? I suppose that such insults to my person were taught to him by others among this upper-class, snobbish, rude, and idiotic group of Prussian Generals and Princes! Because of them, the Empire is fallen! Because of one man's fear of glory, we are to lose this war? No, I shall not leave Berlin. I shall stay here until the communists bust down the door to the bunker, and then I shall kill myself, gentlemen.

Steiner was captured by the British at Lüneburg. He faced charges at Nuremberg, but they were dropped and he was released in 1948.

Hitler decreed that the *SS-Totenkopfverbände* (SS-TV) was to join the SS-VT. The SS-VT had been established by Theodor Eicke in 1936, using concentration camp guards. By and large, it was an army of thugs. In 1937, Eicke declared that it belonged 'neither to the army nor the police nor to the *Verfügungstruppe*'. The SS-VT was now growing apace. By April 1938, it consisted of four regiments which comprised three storm battalions with three infantry companies, one machine-gun company

and medical, communication and transportation units. While the *Leibstandarte* had marched alongside the *Wehrmacht* during the *Anschluss*, two battalions of the *SS-Totenkopfverbände* had been stationed with three battalions of the SS-VT during the occupation of the Sudetenland.

On 19 August 1939, the 8,000 men of the SS-TV were mobilized alongside 18,000 of the SS-VT. Himmler bade farewell to his troops with the words: 'SS men, I expect you to do more than your duty.' In other words, do or die.

Even in action the SS-VT remained a political arm of the Nazi Party, funded by the Ministry of the Interior. However, in Poland the SS-VT was under the authority of the army, who

The face of a fiend? Theodor Eicke ran a regime of 'inflexible harshness', based on hatred of those who fell foul of Nazi ideolology

The SS-VT was established by Eicke, using concentration camp guards. By and large it was an army of thugs

were less than impressed. Its members were poorly trained and they recklessly exposed themselves to danger on the battlefield, sustaining proportionally higher casualties than the *Wehrmacht*. One army general complained that the *Leibstandarte SS Adolf Hitler* fired aimlessly in all directions and routinely set fire to Polish villages. At one point Sepp Dietrich had to be rescued by an infantry regiment when his SS men were surrounded by the Poles near Pabianice. Unsurprisingly, the army recommended that the SS-VT be disbanded.

But Himmler argued that the SS-VT had not been properly equipped by the *Wehrmacht* to carry out its objectives. Moreover, it had been hampered by being parcelled out piecemeal to army units rather than being kept together as a single formation. For once he was right. Hitler showed that he agreed with Himmler by reorganizing the *Germania*, *Deutschland* and *Der Führer* regiments into the *SS-Verfügungs* Division, which would fight under the command of the army. But he held back the now motorized *Leibstandarte* and other elements of the SS-VT to form the nucleus of a new division. The SS-TV would become the *SS-Totenkopf* Division and the *SS*

Polizei Division would be formed by drafting in members of the uniformed national police force.

Almost overnight, the formation that the army had wanted to disband had increased in numbers from 26,000 to over 100,000. Hitler also ordered the formation of a motorized artillery battalion to support the new divisions, though the army was slow to supply them with guns. In an effort to keep his troops out of the hands of the *Wehrmacht*, Himmler persuaded Hitler to institute special SS courts, so that SS men would not be subject to the jurisdiction of the army. An SS man had already been court-martialled for shooting 50 Polish Jews. A totally trivial offence, in Himmler's eyes.

The *Waffen-SS* gets its name

Himmler then called on the organizational abilities of Gottlob Berger. While serving as an officer in the First World War, Berger had been seriously wounded and had been awarded the Iron Cross. He then joined the *Freikorps* and the Nazi Party in 1922. After serving in the SA, he joined the SS in 1936 and was a co-author of Himmler's pamphlet *Der Untermensch* ('subhumans'), which purported to explain why Jews, gypsies, Poles and Slavs were less than human. However, Himmler was happy enough to recruit non-ethnic Germans for the *Waffen-SS*. Berger was sent to put down an uprising in Slovakia in August 1944 and was then put in charge of a prisoner-of-war camp. He was acquitted of ordering death marches at the end of the war, but was sentenced to 25 years' imprisonment for his part in the Holocaust. This was reduced to ten years because he had refused to kill the VIP prisoners who were held in Colditz Castle despite direct orders from Hitler. He was released in 1951.

Berger began recruiting support formations to be manned by the SS and Himmler remained

Nicknamed 'The Almighty Gottlob', Gottlob Berger (left) was a brilliant organizer and a major force behind the expansion of the *Waffen-SS*

in command of the reserves, who could then be used for 'police activities' and other 'special duties'. Himmler had problems equipping his new formations because the *Wehrmacht* was more concerned with supplying its own men, so he set up his own SS Procurement Office under Heinrich Gärtner. Gärtner presented a shopping list containing hundreds of artillery pieces, thousands of small arms and millions of rounds of ammunition direct to armaments minister Fritz Todt. Todt was happy to comply

if the SS would provide 25,000 Polish workers for the Reich's munitions factories. Gärtner even went direct to the manufacturers in his search for supplies. This was one step too far for the *Wehrmacht*, who tried to put a stop to Gärtner's private supply system. Although Himmler had been thwarted in his ambition to make his growing army totally independent, he began calling it the *Waffen-SS*, or 'Weapons SS'. It was certainly that. Adolf Hitler confirmed the name in a speech made in 1940.

overall command of General Sepp Dietrich, was attached to the army's 227th Infantry Division. Its task was to form the vanguard of the ground advance into the Netherlands. The target of the *SS-Verfügungs* Division was the Dutch central front and Rotterdam, while the *SS-Totenkopf* and *SS-Polizei* Divisions were held in reserve.

First of all the *Der Führer* Regiment moved up to the Dutch border, while the remainder of the *SS-Verfügungs* Division – that is, the *Deutschland* and *Germania* Regiments – stayed behind the line in Münster, awaiting the order to invade the Netherlands.

On 10 May the *Leibstandarte* overwhelmed the Dutch border guards and spearheaded the German advance into the Netherlands, while the *Der Führer* advanced towards Utrecht. The following day, the rest of the *SS-Verfügungs* Division crossed into the Netherlands and headed towards Rotterdam. Stiff resistance stalled the advance and Hitler ordered the terror bombing of the city. Within 15 minutes the city centre was demolished and 800 inhabitants were dead. Two hours later, the city's defence force surrendered.

When the *Leibstandarte* marched into the city, General Kurt Student, commander of the Paratroop Division, was setting up his command post in the former Dutch military headquarters. The Dutch troops were disarming in accordance with the surrender agreement but the *Leibstandarte* still turned its machine guns on them. Surprised, General Student rushed to his window to find out what was happening, but a stray bullet hit him in the head, putting him out of action for eight months.

Having almost killed one of Germany's finest generals, the *Leibstandarte* swept on through Delft, even though the Dutch commander-in-chief had already capitulated.

The Battle of France

The three SS divisions – *SS-Verfügungs*, *SS-Totenkopf* and *SS-Polizei* – and the *Leibstandarte SS Adolf Hitler* spent the winter of 1939 and the spring of 1940 training and preparing for the invasion of France. They were to be part of *Fall Gelb* (Case Yellow), one of the two main German operations. Their aim was to cut off and surround the Allied units that had advanced into Belgium.

In May the SS divisions moved up to their starting positions. The *Leibstandarte*, under the

The city centre of Rotterdam with only the famous Laurenskerk still standing after the visit by 90 bombers from *Kampfgeschwader 54*

They captured 3,500 Dutch prisoners of war and reached The Hague before they heard the news of the Netherlands' formal surrender.

Meanwhile, the British armoured forces were fighting back. On 21 May units of the British 1st Army Tank Brigade, supported by the 50th (Northumbrian) Infantry Division, counterattacked in the Battle of Arras, the only tank battle in France. *SS-Totenkopf* had underestimated the opposition to its cost. Its standard anti-tank gun, the 3.7cm (1.5in) PaK 36, was found to be no match for the British Matilda tank.

After the Dutch surrender, the *Leibstandarte* moved south to France. As part of the XIX Panzer Corps under the command of General Heinz Guderian, it took up a position 15 miles (24km) southwest of Dunkirk along the line of the Aa canal. On the evening of 24 May, Hitler ordered the advance to halt. It was one of his most inexplicable decisions. The Allied defeat would have been complete if Guderian had not stopped. As it was, the British Expeditionary Force was trapped. The *Leibstandarte* Division paused for the night, as Hitler had ordered, but across the canal Allied observers on top of the 230ft (70m) heights could rain down shells on Dietrich's men. So on the following morning Dietrich defied Hitler's orders and continued the advance. III Battalion crossed the canal and took the height beyond, driving off the British artillery observers. Instead of being censured for disobeying Hitler's orders, Dietrich was awarded the Knight's Cross.

The same day the British attacked the German bridgehead at St Venant, forcing the *SS-Verfügungs* Division to retreat. It was the

Le Paradis massacre

ON 27 May 1940, soldiers of the 2nd Battalion of the Royal Norfolk Regiment became detached from their regiment. They occupied a farmhouse outside the village of Le Paradis in the Pas-de-Calais and defended it against the men of the *SS-Totenkopf* Division. When they ran out of ammunition the 99 survivors surrendered to the 14th Company of the *SS-Totenkopf* Division under the command of SS Captain Fritz Knöchlein. Instead of being taken prisoner they were machine-gunned and any survivors were finished off with bayonets. A group of French civilians was forced to bury the bodies the next day. But two men of the regiment, Private William O'Callaghan and Private Albert Pooley, escaped by hiding in a pigsty. They were later captured by the *Wehrmacht*, but they survived the war and so were able to testify against Knöchlein at his trial in 1948. He was sentenced to death and was hanged in Hamburg on 28 January 1949. No other German soldiers or officers were prosecuted for their roles in the massacre. It was later discovered that 21 soldiers from the Royal Scots Regiment were also massacred in Le Paradis at around the same time.

first time any SS unit had been forced to give up the ground it had captured. But nothing was going to stop the Germans' relentless advance. On 27 May the *Deutschland* Regiment commanded by Felix Steiner reached the defensive line on the Lys Canal at Merville. Its tanks forced a bridgehead across the river and waited for the *SS-Totenkopf* Division to cover their flank and provide support. However, a unit of British tanks arrived first. The *Deutschland* Regiment was almost overrun, but it managed to hold on until the anti-tank guns of the *Totenkopf Panzerjäger* platoon drove the British armour away. Meanwhile the troops of the 14th Company of the *SS-Totenkopf* Division were committing an atrocity at Le Paradis (see box).

On 28 May Dietrich's staff car was raked with fire from an isolated British outpost. Dietrich and his adjutant scrambled for the safety of a ditch when the bullets ignited the fuel tank. However, the burning petrol ran into the ditch and they had to smear their bodies with mud to protect themselves from the heat. They remained in the ditch, under fire, for five hours until III Battalion arrived to rescue them.

The *Leibstandarte* had just taken Wormhoudt, only 10 miles (16km) from Dunkirk, where it had been responsible for the Wormhoudt massacre.

By 30 May the British were cornered at Dunkirk, leaving the SS divisions free to continue their advance into France. The *Leibstandarte* soon reached Saint-Étienne, 250 miles (400km) south of Paris, which meant that it had advanced further into France than any other unit. On the following day the French surrendered. Hitler was particularly pleased with the performance of the *Leibstandarte*, telling its men: 'Henceforth it will be an honour for you, who bear my name, to lead every German attack.' And during a speech to the Reichstag on 19 July 1940, he praised 'the valiant divisions and regiments of the *Waffen-SS*'. They were, he said, 'superiority personified, inspired by a fierce will'. Excerpts of the speech were printed as a propaganda leaflet under the headline 'A last appeal to reason' and were dropped over England.

Hitler gave his permission for the *Waffen-SS* to form its own high command, the Command Office of the *Waffen-SS*, within the SS-Leader-

Wormhoudt massacre

AFTER fighting a rearguard action during the retreat towards Dunkirk, men from the 2nd Battalion Royal Warwickshire Regiment, the Cheshire Regiment and the Royal Artillery, together with a group of French soldiers, were overrun by the advancing Germans. They surrendered on 28 May 1940, expecting to be dealt with according to the Geneva Convention. Instead, they were taken to a barn near Wormhoudt. When there were almost 100 men inside, 12 soldiers from the *SS-Leibstandarte Adolf Hitler* threw stick-grenades into the building, killing many of the prisoners. Ten survivors, in two groups of five, were then taken outside and shot in the back. Eighty men were killed in all. Fifteen survivors were eventually found by a regular German army unit and their wounds were treated before they were sent to prisoner-of-war camps. Postwar testimony revealed that soldiers of II Battalion under the command of Captain Wilhelm Mohnke had carried out the atrocity, but Mohnke never faced a trial for the massacre. The case was re-examined in 1988 and 1993, but the German prosecutor decided that there was insufficient evidence to bring charges. Mohnke died in August 2001.

SS units reached the English Channel in May 1940. Here they are organizing captured French troops for dispatch to POW camps

ship Main Office (SS-FHA), Himmler's own high command. It was put in charge of the SS-VT (the *Leibstandarte* and the *Verfügungs* Division, renamed *Reich*) and the armed SS-TV regiments (the *Totenkopf* Division together with several independent *Totenkopf-Standarten*).

Foreigners in the Waffen-SS

Despite Hitler's words of praise, the recruiting offices held up the processing of 15,000 SS recruits. Gottlob Berger then came up with an idea. Why not set up recruiting offices in the territories they had already occupied where they could tap into a reserve of 'the German and Germanic population not available to the *Wehrmacht*'? The SS had already accepted foreign recruits with 'Nordic' ancestry, including five from the United States, three from Sweden and 45 from Switzerland, so the concept was not so outlandish. Even so, Hitler had reservations about recruiting foreigners. He had envisaged the SS as an elite formation pulsing with the best German blood. However, he was planning to attack the Soviet Union and recruiting foreigners was a good way of expanding the SS without taking men from the *Wehrmacht*. Himmler and Berger also argued that it would be better for young radicals in occupied territories to join the SS than the resistance. Hitler eventually gave his permission to form a new SS division of foreign nationals under the command of German officers.

By June 1941, Danish and Norwegian volunteers had formed the *SS-Nordland* Regiment, with Dutch and Flemish volunteers

An SS patrol in Brussels near the Palais de Justice, Brussels – the Germans invaded Belgium and the Netherlands in the summer of 1940

constituting the *SS-Westland* Regiment. Together with *Germania*, transferred from the *Reich* Division, they became the *SS-Wiking* Division. Volunteers came forward in such numbers that the SS had to open a new training camp solely for foreign recruits at Sennheim in Alsace-Lorraine.

Not all of the recruits were happy. They had signed up as anti-Bolshevik patriots and had been told that their native traditions would be respected. But the Flemish Catholics who had signed up in Belgium found that they were not allowed to celebrate Mass in camp. They were also shocked to be derided by their sergeants as a 'nation of idiots' and a 'race of gypsies'. But Himmler sought to mollify them by exchanging their old captured arms with new weapons manufactured in Germany.

THE BRITS WHO FOUGHT FOR HITLER

The British Free Corps was perhaps the most bizarre *Waffen-SS* unit. It was made up of a number of British and Dominion prisoners of war, who had been recruited by the Nazis. The force seems to have attracted about 60 members during the period of its existence, though some only served for a few days. However, its strength never seems to have risen above 27 at any one time.

The BFC was the brainchild of John Amery, the son of Leo Amery, Winston Churchill's secretary of state for India. Amery was a fan of National Socialism who saw Jewish-Soviet plotters round every corner. In France after the armistice, he made a number of pro-Nazi speeches in Paris before going off to Berlin, where he put forward his British anti-Bolshevik

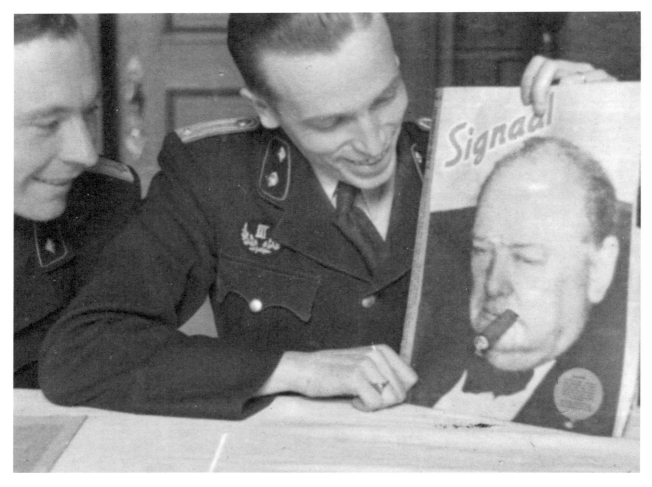

Dutch SS volunteers with their version of propaganda magazine *Signal*, which was published fortnightly in 25 languages across Europe

legion idea. He called it the 'British Legion of St George'. The Nazis were understandably keen on the idea, so Amery staged a recruiting drive in the prisoner-of-war camps. He claimed that he could recruit a brigade of 1,500 fighting men, but the Germans were not so sure.

Months later, he had only come up with four volunteers: an elderly academic named Logio, Maurice Tanner, Oswald Job and Kenneth Berry, a 17-year-old deckhand on the *SS Cymbeline*, which was sunk. Logio was released and Job was recruited by German intelligence and trained as a spy. He was caught while trying to get into England. Only Berry would actually join.

The *Waffen-SS* decided that they could do better themselves, so they dropped Amery and came up with a new recruitment plan.

They created two 'holiday camps' near Berlin, where English-speaking guards would gather information about likely recruits once they were relaxed and off their guard. Quartermaster Sergeant John Brown was put in charge of the operation. A former member of the British Union of Fascists, he had been captured at Dunkirk. The Nazis did not know that he was a double agent.

Also in the camp were two genuine pro-Nazi recruits, Thomas Haller Cooper and Roy Courlander.

Cooper was also a member of the BUF. He called himself Boettcher, the German equivalent of his name. He had been visiting Germany, his mother's birthplace, when war was declared in 1939. At that point, joining the *Waffen-SS* had been the line of least resistance.

After being injured in battle, he had received the Wounded Badge in silver, the only Briton to be awarded a German combat decoration.

Courlander had been captured while serving with the New Zealand army in Greece. His mother was English and his father was a Lithuanian Jew.

Two hundred British prisoners of war then turned up at the camp. Delighted at their windfall, Cooper and Courlander attempted to make as many converts as possible, while Brown tried to subvert the exercise. But out of the first batch they only managed to recruit one man, Alfred Vivian Minchin, a merchant seaman from the SS *Empire Ranger* that had been sunk off the coast of Norway.

Meanwhile two more recruits arrived – Francis George MacLardy of the Royal Army Medical Corps, who had been captured in Belgium, and Edwin Martin of the Canadian Essex Scottish Regiment, who had been captured at Dieppe in 1942 – bringing the strength of the Legion of St George to seven.

Weary of waiting, the Germans decided to try a different tack. A new camp was set up at Luckenwalde, where freshly captured, disorientated prisoners were brought, rather than men who had spent months or years in captivity. First they were maltreated and then they were interviewed by Germans pretending to be Americans, or other British prisoners of

Prisoners were maltreated and then interviewed by Germans pretending to be Americans or British POWs

war. If that failed, they were threatened with solitary confinement. This approach brought in a further 14 recruits, including Trooper John Wilson of 3 Commando and some members of the Argyll and Sutherland Highlanders. The volunteers were told that they were going to join thousands of their countrymen. Some were fascists but the others were just pretending in order to gain their freedom.

Like Brown, Edwin Martin had also joined to disrupt the operation. Thanks to his efforts the number of men in the Legion of St George had fallen to eight by December 1943. SS Captain Walter Roepke, formerly with the *SS-Allgemeine* and the *SS-Wiking* Division, was then put in charge. He felt that the Legion of St George sounded too religious. Himmler suggested the British Legion but that name had already been taken, so Roepke came up with the name 'British Free Corps'. If he managed to attract 30 recruits the unit would be commissioned as an infantry platoon, so that was his primary aim.

Under pressure from the recruits, Roepke then made certain concessions. The BFC would be under British command; its members would not be branded with the SS blood-group tattoo; they did not have to swear an oath of loyalty to Hitler; they were not subject to German military law; and they would not be used in any action against British or Commonwealth forces or used for intelligence gathering.

However, they would receive pay equal to German soldiers of their rank.

Meanwhile, Roepke put in an optimistic order for 800 SS uniforms with BFC insignia. There were three lions on the collar patches and there was a cuff band with 'British Free Corps' on it and a Union Flag arm badge. The Union Flag badge was attached to the left sleeve, just under the German eagle. 'Look, the eagle is sh***ing on the flag,' said one recruit. Eventually, permission to switch the Union Flag to the right sleeve had to be sought from Himmler.

Another potential saboteur then arrived in the form of Private Thomas Freeman of No. 7 Commando of Layforce. At this stage Roepke surveyed his pitiful force and came up with a new recruiting plan. All of the members of the BFC were sent back to their original camps on a recruiting mission, but they only managed to come back with six further volunteers. Two of these were John Leister, son of a German whose family had Nazi ties, and Eric Pleasants, a former member of the BUF. Both of them were pacifists who had been sent as agricultural workers to Jersey. Having failed to escape when the islands were occupied, they had joined the BFC in the hope of getting access to better food, alcohol and women.

Successive recruiting drives dragged the unit's strength up to 23. Fearing that their numbers might reach the crucial 30, which would propel them into action, Freeman and a like-minded comrade persuaded 14 other members to request a transfer back to their prisoner-of-war camps. The two troublemakers were charged with mutiny and sent to a penal *Stalag*. Freeman escaped and was repatriated by the Soviets in March 1945.

Wilson talked the Germans into making him senior NCO, while Cooper tried to instil SS-style discipline into his men. This did not go down well with the lackadaisical Brits. At that stage, four more recruits arrived. Three had been coerced into joining and one had made his German girlfriend pregnant, which was a capital offence. Getting girls pregnant was an SS monopoly!

The Germans thought they were making headway when they hooked Lieutenant William Shearer, the only officer to join the BFC. Although he had been recruited from a mental hospital, he seemed to know what the BFC was all about. His captors were quickly disillusioned. Not only did he refuse to put on the BFC uniform, he would not even leave his room. After a few weeks, he was returned to the mental hospital, before being repatriated on medical grounds.

The D-Day landings had been a success but there was no let-up for the BFC recruits. SS Major Vivian Stranders joined as second in command. Originally British, he took German nationality when he joined the Nazi Party in 1932. After the war began, he was posted to the *Waffen-SS*, who used him as an expert on British affairs. At that point, MacLardy left the BFC to join the *Waffen-SS* medical unit and Courlander joined the war correspondent unit *SS-Standarte Kurt Eggers*. BFC men Walter Purdy, John Leister and Francis Maton also joined. Courlander could see the sense in getting out while the going was good, so he took a companion and jumped on to a railway train that was bound for Brussels. Once there, they handed themselves over to the British. As soon as they had gone, two more men took their places. Once again they had been caught *in flagrante* with a couple of German women.

In October 1944, the straggling band of recruits was sent to the *Waffen-SS* Pioneer School in Dresden to be trained as combat engineers. However, all attempts to fashion the

YOUR PLACE IS HERE!

Few army units anywhere can have been as unpopular as the British Free Corps, who were desperate to recruit anyone that they could

BFC into a fighting unit were abandoned when Stranders successfully ousted Roepke, replacing him with SS First Lieutenant Walther Kuhlich, who had been wounded on the front line.

Cooper had been accused of anti-Nazi acts by the other BFC men so he was returned to the *Leibstandarte SS Adolf Hitler* as a military policeman. Wilson was now in charge of recruiting. Although he was more interested in womanizing, he tried to get men who had left the BFC to return. Meanwhile, Pleasants wooed Annelise, Kuhlich's secretary, marrying her in February 1945. Morale slumped when training for the Eastern Front resumed, with men getting drunk and going AWOL. Five more recruits joined, including two South Africans, taking the force's strength up to 27. Two had wanted to join the *SS-Totenkopf* Division until they were swayed by Kuhlich. Then six Maoris volunteered, which would have put the unit's numbers over the magic 30, but they were rejected because the SS was a 'whites-only' organization.

Then six Maoris volunteered, but they were rejected because the SS was a 'whites-only' organization

While Wilson was away, Hugh Cowie, a Gordon Highlander, took over as senior NCO. During the bombing of Dresden in February 1945, a few members of the BFC tried to escape, but they were given away by someone's girlfriend. The entire BFC was arrested, but two of them managed to make their escape. Everyone else was taken to Berlin. As the Allies closed in, a sympathetic officer provided three BFC members with British uniforms. Another managed to get transferred, because his girlfriend was connected with *SS-Standarte Kurt Eggers*.

Kuhlich gave the rest of the BFC a choice – fight or be sent to an isolation camp. They all chose to fight, so they were sent to join the III (Germanic) SS Panzer Corps, taking off their BFC insignia on the way. They spent a month on the front line. Cooper was then serving with the III (Germanic) SS Panzer Corps. He took SS Lieutenant-General Felix Steiner to inspect the BFC, but they were found to be of such dubious combat value that they were pulled from the line. Steiner was also concerned about the postwar legal consequences of using prisoners of war in action, because it was a clear violation of the Geneva Convention.

The relieved group of recruits then returned to Berlin, where they tried to locate their Red Cross parcels – they were still technically prisoners of war. At that point the colourful, if dubious, SS Captain Douglas Berneville-Claye appeared. Having been drummed out of the RAF, he had talked his way into the SAS. He was captured in North Africa and sent to Oflag 79 (a prison camp for Allied officers), but he had been released after switching sides. Cooper was not impressed by Berneville-Claye's credentials. Rightly so. He soon commandeered a car and went off to surrender to the Allies.

A couple of the BFC men saw action at the end of the war. Wilhelm 'Bob' Rossler was with the *Nordland* Division during the Battle of Berlin and Roy Courlander also seems to have been there. He is said to have put a Soviet tank out of action. The rest of the group accompanied Steiner when he sallied forth to surrender to the British.

Meanwhile, Hugh Cowie and his fellow would-be escapees seized control of their isolation camp. Heavily armed, they made their way west and surrendered to the United States Ninth Army at Schwerin.

Amery, Cooper and Walter Purdy stood trial for high treason alongside the propagandist William Joyce ('Lord Haw-Haw'). Amery and Joyce were hanged while Cooper and Purdy's sentences were commuted to life imprisonment. Cooper was released in 1953 and Purdy was freed in the following year. The rest were dealt with under military law. MacLardy was sentenced to life imprisonment, reduced on appeal to fifteen years, Cowie was sentenced to fifteen years' imprisonment but was released after seven years, Wilson was sent to prison for ten years and Berry, the very first recruit, served just nine months. Courland was court-martialled by the New Zealand forces, who sentenced him to fifteen years in prison, but he served only seven of them. Freeman successfully defended himself on all charges, and was acquitted. Berneville-Claye was as slippery as ever. After he was acquitted due to lack of evidence he served another year in the army before being discharged for theft.

In mid-1946, MI5 discovered that three former BFC members, who had been demobilized, had escaped punishment. It was too late to court-martial them, so they were summoned to MI5 headquarters and told not to do it again. No doubt they gladly agreed.

Pleasants and his wife Annelise escaped from Berlin through the sewers. He claimed to have killed two Russian soldiers with his bare hands along the way. The couple made their way to Annelise's parents in Dresden, where Pleasants joined a circus as a strong man, but they were arrested in 1946. Although Pleasants confessed to being a member of the SS, the Cold War was under way and he was forced to admit to a charge of spying for the United Kingdom. He was sentenced to 25 years in a labour camp in Arctic Russia, but he was released in 1953, after the death of Stalin. His wife was never heard of again.

AMERICANS IN THE *WAFFEN-SS*

Although there was a British Free Corps there was no corresponding American unit. True enough, there was the American Free Corps, also known as the George Washington Brigade, but it was a fictitious unit of the *Waffen-SS* made up for propaganda purposes. But that did not mean that there were no Americans in the *Waffen-SS*. A number of Americans fought alongside the Germans, but they were spread out among different units. However, most of them died and little was done to investigate their cases. A selection of American *Waffen-SS* recruits follows:

Andy Beneschan

Born 1 September 1918 in New York, he was an SS sergeant before being killed in action in Bosnia on 16 April 1945.

Charles Braschwitz

Born 17 August 1911 in New Jersey, he became a sergeant in the *SS-Polizei* before being killed in action on 7 May 1945 at Laibach, Slovenia.

Bosnian Muslim SS volunteers pray to Mecca in 1943 – Himmler accepted them into the SS fold as 'descendants of 6th-century Goths'

Peter Delaney (aka Pierre de la Ney du Vair)
Born in Louisiana, he is believed to have served in the French collaborationist *Légion des Volontaires Français* and as an SS captain in the *SS-Standarte Kurt Eggers* before being killed in 1945.

Lucas Diel
Born 28 December 1912 in New York, he was an SS corporal before dying in Hungary on 9 December 1944.

Andreas Hauser
Born 30 August 1893 in Los Angeles, he was an SS lance corporal until he was killed in action on 18 January 1945 at Welikij in Ukraine.

Charles MacDonald
Born 7 May 1922 in Buffalo, New York, he reportedly rose to become an SS second lieutenant before being killed in action in Estonia on 14 March 1944.

Martin James Monti
Born 1910 in St Louis of an Italian-Swiss father and a German mother, he was a second lieutenant in the US Army Air Corps before he went AWOL in October 1944. He flew to Milan in a stolen plane and worked as a propaganda broadcaster under the pseudonym Martin Wiethaupt. Later he met Peter Delaney, who probably arranged for him to enter the *Waffen-SS* as an SS second lieutenant in the *SS-Standarte Kurt Eggers*. At the end of the war he returned to Italy

where he surrendered to the United States forces, claiming that the SS uniform he was wearing had been given to him by partisans. He was charged only with desertion and was sentenced to 15 years' hard labour. His other crimes had not come to light. His sentence was commuted and he rejoined the United States Air Corps, but in 1948 he was discharged and picked up by the FBI. He was charged with treason and sentenced to 25 years' imprisonment, but he was paroled in 1960.

Edwin or Erwin Peter
Born 12 March 1918 in New York, he rose to become an SS company sergeant major before being killed in action on 2 July 1941 in Latvia.

Raymond George Rommelspacher
Born 30 May 1926 in Chicago, he was an SS-Grenadier and was killed in action on 6 October 1944 in Normandy.

Going to Mussolini's aid

At the beginning of 1941, the *Polizei* division had been brought under SS Leadership Main Office (FHA) control, although it would not be formally merged into the *Waffen-SS* until 1942. At the same time the *Totenkopfstandarten* – apart from the three regiments constituting the *Totenkopf* Division – lost their death's head designation and insignia and were reclassified as *SS-Infanterie* or *SS-Kavallerie* regiments. The 11th Regiment was transferred into the *Reich* Division to replace the *Germania* and the remainder were grouped into three independent brigades and a battle group in Norway.

By the spring, the *Waffen-SS* had grown to be the equivalent of six or seven divisions.

It comprised the *Reich, Totenkopf, Wiking* and *Polizei* divisions, the battle group (later division) *Nord* and the *Leibstandarte*, along with the 1 SS Infantry, 2 SS Infantry and SS Cavalry brigades. They were being prepared for the attack on the Soviet Union when events took an unexpected turn after Mussolini's invasion of Greece went horribly wrong. 'Il Duce' was now in deep trouble, so Hitler had no choice but to go to his aid.

Reich was ordered to leave France for Romania, and the *Leibstandarte*, reinforced to full brigade strength, was sent to Bulgaria. There was little love lost between the SS and the *Wehrmacht* as they jostled on the traffic-choked roads. On one occasion, an SS officer threatened to open fire on an army convoy if it tried to overtake his column and on another the lead vehicle of an army column was held up at gunpoint to clear the road for the SS.

The fighting started on the morning of 6 April. Attached to the XL Panzer Corps, the *Leibstandarte* advanced west and then south from Bulgaria into the mountains. By 9 April it had reached Prilep, 30 miles (48km) from the Greek border. Further north the *SS-Reich*, with the XLI Panzer Corps, crossed the Romanian border and advanced on Belgrade, the Yugoslav capital. On 12 April the shattered city surrendered. The Yugoslav army followed suit a few days later.

Then on 10 April the *Leibstandarte* crossed into Greece and came face to face with the 6th Australian Division at the Klidi Pass. For 48 hours the two sides fought for control of the heights, often engaging in bloody hand-to-hand combat. Eventually the *Leibstandarte* captured the pass, which allowed the German army to advance into the Greek interior. The victory finally elicited grudging praise from the *Wehrmacht*. The order of the day from General

Belgrade after its visit by the Luftwaffe on Operation Punishment, 1941, a terror bombing ordered by Hitler in which more than 2,000 died

Georg Stumme, commander of XL Panzer Corps, commended the *Leibstandarte* for its 'unshakable offensive spirit'.

'The present victory signifies for the *Leibstandarte* a new and imperishable page of honour in its history,' Stumme went on. 'Forward for *Führer, Volk und Reich.*'

The *Leibstandarte* continued its advance on 13 May, but the reconnaissance battalion under the command of Kurt Meyer faltered when it came under heavy machine-gun fire from the

Greek army defending the Klisura Pass. Meyer ordered his men forward. When there was no response he grabbed a hand grenade and waved it in the air.

'Everyone looked thunderstruck at me as I brandished the grenade, pulled the pin and rolled it precisely behind the last man,' he recalled. 'Never again did I witness such a concerted leap forward as at that second. As if bitten by tarantulas, we dived around the rock spur and into a fresh crater.'

elements had been added at the start of the Russian campaign, it remained effectively a reinforced brigade.

Operation Barbarossa

With the southern flank secured, Hitler could go ahead with Operation Barbarossa, the invasion of the Soviet Union. At 0530 hours on 22 June 1941, the German ambassador in Moscow went to see foreign minister Molotov. He delivered a declaration of war. The reason – or excuse – was 'gross and repeated violations' of the Molotov–Ribbentrop Pact. If Stalin had read *Mein Kampf* he might have been prepared. Hitler had announced his intention to invade the Soviet Union back in 1926: 'Germany's future has to lie in the acquisition of land in the east at the expense of Russia.'

The German ambassador's words were a mere formality, because a huge German army was already pouring across the Russian border on a 900-mile (1,450km) front from the Baltic to the Black Sea.

The *Wehrmacht* attacked in three army groups. The *SS-Totenkopf* and *SS-Polizei* divisions were attached to Army Group North. They advanced through the Baltic states and on to Leningrad. The *SS-Reich* division, which became 2 *SS-Das Reich* that autumn, was with Army Group Centre when it headed towards Moscow and the *SS-Wiking* Division and the *Leibstandarte* were with Army Group South. Their targets were Ukraine and the city of Kiev.

A week later the *SS-Nord* Division joined XXXVI Corps, which consisted of both German and Finnish troops. Confident of success they poured across the border into Finland, which the Red Army had taken the previous year under the Molotov–Ribbentrop Pact. The advance came to a juddering halt when they came up against a powerful Soviet force at

Thus emboldened, the *Leibstandarte* routed the defenders and captured 1,000 prisoners of war at the cost of six dead and nine wounded. On the following day, Meyer captured the town of Kastoria and bagged another 11,000 prisoners of war. By 20 May the *Leibstandarte* had cut off the retreating divisions of the Greek Epirus–Macedonian army. The Greeks surrendered to Sepp Dietrich while shouting 'Heil Germania!' and 'Heil Hitler!'. Three days later Greece capitulated and the British fled. As a reward the *Leibstandarte* was promoted to a full motorized division. But while a few additional

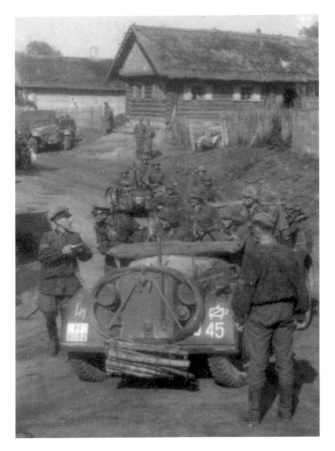

Waffen-SS division *Das Reich* advances through the Soviet Union
during the summer of 1941

Salla, near the Russian border with Finland.
Disorientated by the thick forests and the heavy
smoke from forest fires, the division's units
disintegrated. Three hundred of the invading
troops were killed and 400 were wounded in
the first two days of the invasion. However,
over the winter of 1941–2 the division was
reinforced from the general pool of *Waffen-SS*
recruits. The replacements were younger and
better trained than the SS-men of the original
formation, who had been largely drawn from
the *Totenkopfstandarten* of concentration camp
guards.

The war in the Soviet Union proceeded
well for Germany at first, but then came the
rasputitza, the autumn rains that turned the
roads into quagmires. In the south, a Soviet
counter-attack forced the Germans out of
Rostov, Germany's first major reverse on the
Eastern Front. By late October, the *Leibstandarte*

was at half strength because of enemy action
and the dysentery that swept through its ranks.
Das Reich had lost 60 per cent of its strength,
but the struggle had barely begun. Hanging
low over the invaders was the bloody spectre
of the Battle of Moscow. On 1 December,
Hitler ordered an all-out attack on the capital,
but the Germans ground to a halt in sub-zero
temperatures, within sight of the city's onion
domes. On 6 December, the Red Army counterattacked, driving the Germans back 40 miles
(64km). *Das Reich* suffered crushing losses. Of
the 2,000 soldiers that had started out with the
Der Führer Regiment, only 35 men were still
standing. The *Waffen-SS* had suffered 43,000
casualties, which meant that around one out
of every four of the German troops had been
killed or wounded. This time the *Wehrmacht*
heaped unstinted praise on the *Waffen-SS*.
Writing to Himmler, Eberhard von Mackensen,
the general commanding III Panzer Corps,
commended the *Leibstandarte* for 'its inner
discipline, its cool daredevilry, its cheerful

As part of the scorched earth policy, two soldiers of the *Waffen-SS*
torch a thatched house near Kharkov in Russia, 1943

The German advance encounters formidable resistance from the weather as this mounted division of the SS pushes towards Moscow

enterprise, its unshakable firmness in a crisis, its exemplary toughness, its camaraderie…' and assured the *Reichsführer* 'that the *Leibstandarte* enjoys an outstanding reputation not only with its superiors but also among its army comrades'. The *Waffen-SS* was also praised by the Russians. A captured Soviet officer said that they had been relieved when the *SS-Wiking* Division had been replaced in the line with a regular army division.

However, it was not just a picture of reckless bravery. The *Waffen-SS* had committed its share of atrocities in Russia, just as it had done in France when it had murdered a number of helpless British prisoners of war. Soviet

prisoners of war had been shot too. And when the people of Ukraine had greeted the Germans as liberators, the *Waffen-SS* had rewarded them with rape and murder.

The 1 SS Infantry and 2 SS Infantry brigades, which had been formed from surplus concentration camp guards from the SS-TV, had joined up with the SS Cavalry Brigade and had moved into the Soviet Union behind the advancing armies. At first they fought Soviet partisans and the isolated units of the Red Army, capturing 7,000 prisoners of war. Then from mid-August 1941 until late 1942 they were assigned to the Reich Main Security Office under Heydrich. The brigades were now

Exhausted soldiers of the *Leibstandarte Adolf Hitler* patrol the battered streets of Kharkov in a Panzer, March 1943

Gustav Lombard commanded the SS cavalry regiment *Florian Geyer*, which had an appalling record for committing atrocities

Watched by members of the *Waffen-SS*, the Labour Service and the Hitler Youth, a man is shot by an *Einsatzgruppe* trooper in the summer of 1941. This famous image was found in the personal album of a captured German soldier; on the back was written a cynical epitaph: 'The Last Jew in Vinnitsa'. (Vinnitsa is a town in Ukraine.)

used for rear area security and policing and, most importantly, they were not under army or *Waffen-SS* command. In the autumn of 1941 they left the anti-partisan role to other units and began assisting the *Einsatzgruppen*. They formed firing parties and participated in the wholesale extermination of the Jewish population of the Soviet Union. By the end of 1941, these three brigades were responsible for the murders of tens of thousands of Jews and other selected victims.

The SS Cavalry Brigade, being more mobile, was particularly culpable. It had first gone into action on 27 July. By 1 August the force was responsible for the deaths of 800 people.

That day, Himmler had a meeting with Erich von dem Bach-Zelewski and the Reich Commissioner for *Ostland* (Germany's eastern territories), Hinrich Lohse. The three men came to a chilling decision, after which Himmler issued a brutal order: 'All Jews must be shot. Drive the female Jews into the swamps.'

On receiving Himmler's command, SS Major Gustav Lombard advised his battalion that 'in future not one male Jew is to remain alive, not one family in the villages'. Five days later, his force's body count had reached 3,000

Concentration camps like Auschwitz lay at the end of the line for anyone who survived their encounters with the SS, including Soviet POWs

'Jews and Partisans'. Over the next weeks, soldiers of 1 SS Cavalry Regiment under Lombard's command murdered an estimated 11,000 Jews and more than 400 Red Army stragglers.

As a youth Lombard often went to stay with his family in America – he was related to the movie actress Carole Lombard, who severed relations with her German family after Hitler's rise to power. After studying modern languages at the University of Missouri, he returned to Germany in 1919, where he worked for American Express and the Chrysler Motor Company in Berlin.

When Hitler came to power in 1933, Lombard joined the Nazi Party and the SS. As a dedicated horseman he was attracted to the *SS-Totenkopf* Cavalry Brigade, which was serving in Poland. He was soon attacking citizens, rather than the enemy, when his unit was ordered to hunt down and kill any

non-German males between the ages of 17 and 60. It seems that the exercise was to everyone's liking, because Lombard's colleagues proudly reported that they had executed 250 people during their deployment.

This would prove to be only a fraction of Lombard's eventual killing tally. A grateful Himmler awarded him the Knight's Cross for his services. Accompanied by the remnants of his last command, the 31st Volunteer Grenadier Division, Lombard went into Soviet captivity at the end of the war. He was released in 1955.

Although he had been a mass murderer of the first degree, Lombard escaped with his life and a relatively light sentence. Other *Waffen-SS* killers faced the gallows when the enormity of their crimes came to light. And as we shall see later, those with the right contacts were spirited abroad at the end of the war, where they would often become respected members of their adopted communities.

CHAPTER SIX
The *SS-Allgemeine*

The SS was reorganized after the creation of the *SS-Verfügungstruppe* (the combat arm) in 1934. The *SS-Totenkopfverbände*, which ran the concentration camps, stayed a separate unit. Opportunists, alcoholics, homosexuals and those of uncertain racial status were purged. Those that remained became the *SS-Allgemeine* (General SS), which soon thrust its claws into every part of German life.

'Fire and move': *Kradschützen* were squads of infantrymen on motorbikes; they were first formed in 1929 after the cavalry was restructured

FOLLOWING ITS reorganization in 1934, the SS comprised three separate forces: the *SS-Allgemeine*, the *SS-Verfügungstruppe* (SS-VT) and the *SS-Totenkopfverbände*. By 1938, *SS-Allgemeine* numbers had risen to 485,000. That figure was boosted by 50,000 when the *SS-Totenkopfverbände*, with the exception of the *SS-Totenkopf* Division, was merged into the *SS-Allgemeine* in May 1939.

In 1935, the *SS-Hauptamt* (SS Head Office or SS-HA) controlled the concentration camps and the SS-VT, as well as the *SS-Allgemeine*. But the SS-VT expanded rapidly, becoming the *Waffen-SS* in 1940. The SS then needed an operational headquarters, so the SS-HA became an administrative office and the SS Leadership

Main Office (SS-FHA) was created. Reporting directly to Himmler, it controlled the Command Department of the *Waffen-SS* and the Command Department of the *SS-Allgemeine*.

Although the *SS-Allgemeine* could be described as the 'General SS', or the political wing of the SS, many of its members were called up into the *Wehrmacht* or the *Waffen-SS* as the war progressed.

Only around 100,000 of its members, such as full-time officers and members of the various domestic departments of the SS, were exempt from military service. Part-time voluntary units were organized by region and district, each district containing a number of *Standarten* or regiments. Some districts even had *Reiterstandarten* – cavalry units.

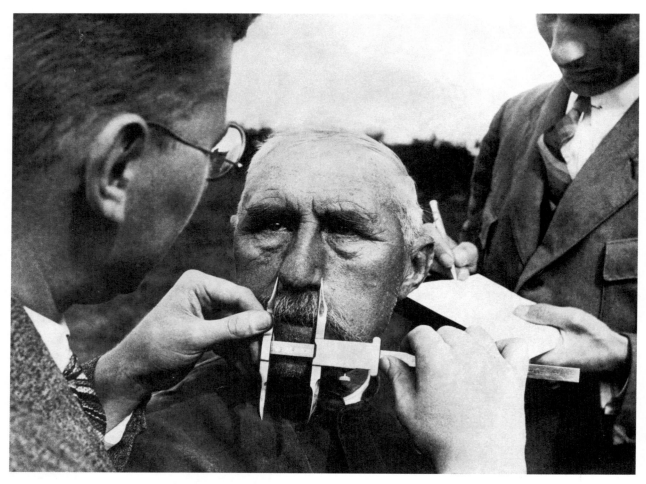

Nazi agents check out a 'suspect citizen' for 'non-Aryan characteristics' with calipers and a tape measure

Diverse roles

The departments of the *SS-Allgemeine* were as various as they were numerous, but the innocuous-sounding Reich Security Head Office (RSHA) perhaps struck terror into the most hearts. It had been created by Himmler through the merger of the Security Service (SD) and the Security Police (SiPo) and its first chief was Reinhard Heydrich.

The SiPo was split into two sections: the Secret State Police (Gestapo) and the Criminal Police (Kripo). After the death of Heydrich, Himmler took over until January 1943. At that point, SS lieutenant-general and general of police Ernst Kaltenbrunner was appointed to fill Heydrich's shoes.

The job of the RSHA was to fight the enemies of the Third Reich – which could be anyone and everyone. However, its main targets included Jews, Roma (gypsies) and other 'racial undesirables', communists, Freemasons, pacifists and Christian activists. Its numerous prisoners would first be sent to the concentration camps, before going on to extermination camps in Poland and the Ukraine. The RSHA also oversaw the *Einsatzgruppen* death squads who murdered their way across Eastern Europe.

Nazi racial policies were administered by the *SS-Allgemeine*'s Race and Settlement Office (RuSHA). Under its aegis, more than 300 men were expelled from the SS in 1937 for contravening Nazi race laws, but in 1940 Himmler reinstated those who had been expelled for marriages that had failed to match Nazi criteria. Perhaps it was because his own marriage had also fallen short of his high ideals. RuSHA shared the task of organizing the Germanization of captured territory with the VoMi (Main Welfare Office for Ethnic Germans) and the office of the RKFDV (Reich Commissioner for the Strengthening of Germanism).

The somewhat bizarre *Ahnenerbe*, the Nazi think tank for investigating ancient history, was also administered by the *SS-Allgemeine*. It was one of Himmler's favourite toys. In June 1941, the organization removed the 900-year-old Bayeux Tapestry so that its Nordic symbolism could be decoded. According to them, it showed the Germanic Franks overwhelming their English enemies. There were also plans to make expeditions to Bolivia, Behistun in Iran and Iceland so that inscriptions, customs and folklore could be examined. It was thought that the Germans' Aryan past could be tracked down to those places. Mummies were studied in the Canary Islands for the same purpose. But the *Ahnenerbe*'s main project was the Aryanization of the conquered territories in Eastern Europe, which Himmler considered would take 20 years.

The *Ahnenerbe* also commissioned medical experiments at Dachau. Because *Luftwaffe* pilots were reaching new heights, some of the camp's inmates were locked in vacuum chambers to see how the human body would react. As well as flying higher, German airmen

Some Dachau inmates were locked in vacuum chambers... or stripped and immersed in tanks of icy water

were crash-landing in icy waters, so prisoners were subjected to similar conditions in a bid to find out if the pilots could survive. Some subjects were stripped and immersed in tanks of icy water, while others were kept outside in freezing weather for up to 14 hours. Attempts were then made to revive them, either by thrusting them into baths of hot water or by using women to stimulate them sexually, a method suggested by Himmler. *Ahnenerbe* scientists also measured Jewish facial features and collected Jewish skulls in an attempt to demonstrate their racial theories.

Less quirky, but much more sinister, was the SS Economic and Administrative Main Office (WVHA), which was responsible for managing finances, supplies and business projects for the *SS-Allgemeine*. It also ran the concentration camps and oversaw the Holocaust. Valuables such as gold watches, rings, currency, gold fillings and glasses were taken from victims when they arrived at the death camps. These items were then sent back to Berlin in WVHA-marked crates, for processing at the Reichsbank. Between August 1942 and January 1945, a total of 76 WVHA consignments had arrived in Berlin, providing hundreds of millions of Reichsmarks for the war effort. The WVHA also aided the economy by providing seemingly limitless amounts of slave labour. These unfortunates were used in the armaments industry and on construction projects such as the building of the Atlantic Wall that fortified the coast from the Arctic to the border of Spain.

After the invasion of the Soviet Union, the SS took operational control of manufacturing and mining in the territories it occupied. It controlled land and forestry, stone quarries, cement works, brick and building materials factories, porcelain and pottery factories, mineral water extraction and bottling, meat processing, bakeries, small arms manufacturing and repair, wooden furniture design and production, herbal medicines, fish processing, the publication of books and magazines on Germanic culture and history, art acquisition and restoration, the forging of ceremonial swords and daggers and the production of military clothing and accessories for the *Wehrmacht* as well as the SS.

The WVHA's economics office controlled the entire production cycle, from the extraction of raw materials to manufacture and distribution, either directly or through a complex network of shell companies that had been set up by WVHA chief SS Lieutenant-General Oswald Pohl.

Himmler's personal headquarters, under Karl Wolff, was also part of the *SS-Allgemeine*, as was the *SS-Personalhauptamt*, the central recording office for the SS (SS-PHA). Its records largely concerned themselves with officers. The Nazis' administrative diligence proved an invaluable resource for the Nuremberg prosecutors. Then there was the SS Leadership Main Office (SS-FHA), which was the operational headquarters of the SS. It was responsible for the administration of *Junkerschulen* officer schools, medical services, logistics and rates of pay, as well as being the administrative and operational headquarters of the *Waffen-SS*. The SS-FHA had priority over all of the other branches of the German armed forces when it

came to the selection of recruits. When Himmler stepped down as SS-FHA chief in 1943, SS Lieutenant-General Hans Jüttner managed the department until the end of the war.

After serving as a lieutenant in the German army during the First World War, Jüttner worked as a salesman. In 1933, he became a university sports teacher in Breslau and then he joined the SA collegiate office. He switched to the SS-VT in 1935, joining the inspection department in Berlin. Promotion was rapid. By 1939, he had become the inspector of reserve troops of the SS-VT Division and from early 1940 he was leading the SS-VT command office. That summer he was appointed chief of staff of the newly created SS-FHA. From 1943, he was in command of all *Waffen-SS* field troops, training and reserve units, schools, command garrisons and headquarters.

On 17 May 1945 Jüttner was taken prisoner by the British and three years later he was sentenced to ten years' imprisonment in a labour camp. This was reduced to four years on appeal. In 1961 he testified for the prosecution in the trial of Holocaust architect Adolf Eichmann and he later became the proprietor of a sanatorium in Bad Tölz, where he died.

Foreign branches

As the Nazi empire spread across Europe, the *SS-Allgemeine* set up the *Germanische SS* (Germanic SS) to oversee the external branches and collaborationist organizations that modelled themselves on the SS. Individuals would apply for membership of the SS and after fulfilling all of the physical and racial requirements they would receive an SS number. Then they would join part-time SS units that performed voluntary drills, undertook ideological instruction, marched in parades and provided security at Party rallies.

THE NETHERLANDS

Foreign branches enforced Nazi racial doctrines in occupied countries and served as local security police alongside the Gestapo and the SD. On 9 June 1940 Hitler ordered Anton Mussert, leader of the Dutch National Socialist Movement, to recruit men for the *Wiking* Division of the *Waffen-SS*. He refused, but the *Wiking* Division was set up anyway. When *Reichskommissar* Arthur Seyss-Inquart threatened to replace Mussert with Dutch fascist politician Meinoud Rost van Tonningen, Mussert was forced to agree to the establishment of the *Nederlandsche SS* under Johannes Hendrik 'Henk' Feldmeijer.

While doing national service in 1931, Feldmeijer met a leader of the recently formed Stormtroopers of the National Socialist Movement in the Netherlands (NSB), which fired his interest in the organization. One of the first 1,000 members, he supported NSB leader Anton Mussert in his bid to be dictator of the Netherlands. He then became a paid member of the party's propaganda department, travelling to Germany, Italy and Scandinavia.

Henk Feldmeijer belonged to the *Völkisch* section of the NSB, which developed ideas about the Germanic heritage of the Dutch and cultivated anti-Semitism. As a result, he had contacts with the German SS behind the back of the NSB. Nevertheless he was appointed commander of Mussert's bodyguard and he trained them as a paramilitary group. In May 1940 he was arrested by the Dutch government, who took him as a prisoner into France when the Nazis invaded. Released when the German army overtook his captors he returned to The Hague, where he met Himmler and Seyss-Inquart. They all held discussions about the Nazification of the Netherlands and the formation of a Dutch SS, the *Nederlandsche SS*.

Hans Jüttner rose swiftly up the Nazi command structure – he later testified for the prosecution in the trial of Adolf Eichmann

As the commander of the *Nederlandsche SS*, Feldmeijer reported directly to Himmler. After exhorting his members to make a direct contribution to the war effort he led by example, serving at the front twice: first as a gunner with the *Leibstandarte SS Adolf Hitler* in Yugoslavia and Greece, and then as flak commander in *SS-Division Wiking* in southern Russia.

In March 1943, he was promoted to the rank of colonel in the *SS-Allgemeine* and a year later he became a captain in the *Waffen-SS*. He also won the Iron Cross Second Class.

Feldmeijer then took part in the reprisals for the liquidations committed by the Dutch resistance. In September 1943, *Sonderkommando-Feldmeijer* killed at least 20 resistance members. However, on 22 February 1945 Feldmeijer met his own end when Allied aircraft strafed his car.

The *Nederlandsche SS* was the Dutch version of the *SS-Allgemeine*. It had the same age, fitness, height, genealogy and character requirements as its German equivalent. Recruits were to have no dishonourable criminal convictions and they had to pledge their unconditional loyalty to all of their superiors. Their uniforms were black, like those of the German SS. The *Nederlandsche SS* was divided into five regional *standaarden* or regiments, with headquarters at Groningen, Arnhem, Amsterdam, The Hague and Eindhoven. There was also a separate

> **In September 1943, Feldmeijer took part in reprisals against the Dutch resistance, killing at least 20 members**

police regiment. The regiments were intended to contain 500 men plus staff but the average *standaard* numbered only 130 men – the rest were siphoned off by the *Waffen-SS*.

The *Nederlandsche SS* was an important recruiting ground, as well as being a reserve. It was also used as a propaganda tool and it helped advance the idea of 'Greater Germany', which would embrace all northern European peoples. This concept was reinforced when the name was changed to *Germaansche SS in Nederland* (Germanic SS in the Netherlands) in November 1942.

As a political formation, the *Germaansche SS in Nederland* helped expand Himmler's empire, but at its peak it only boasted around 7,000 members. However, there was also a Dutch version of the German *SS-Fördernde Mitglieder* (SS-FM), an association of SS supporters who paid a monthly fee. It had a membership of around 4,000. By the end of 1944, with the tide turning against Germany, the *Germaansche SS in Nederland* became an organization that existed only on paper.

FLANDERS

There was a similar formation in Flanders, the Flemish-speaking region of Belgium. Originally called the *Algemeene-SS Vlaanderen*, it was renamed the *Germaansche SS in Vlaanderen* (Germanic SS in Flanders) in 1942. It provided military drill and ideological education, and ran its own newspaper, *De SS-Man*. There was only one *standaard*, or unit, which was divided into four regional *stormbans* (storm units), but there was also a Flemish version of the SS-FM, called the *Beschermde Leden* (BL). The BL had around 4,200 members, who were equally divided between women and men.

During the German occupation of Belgium, opinion regarding the future of Flanders was more or less split between the followers of *DeVlag*, a pro-Nazi organization, and the Flemish National Union (VNV), the largest nationalist movement in Flanders.

DeVlag had been set up by Dr Jef van de Wiele in 1935. Its symbol was the Nazi eagle and swastika combined with the black lion of Flanders. In May 1941, after the German invasion of Belgium, *DeVlag* started to receive support from the SS and was reorganized into a National Socialist organization. This caused a rift with the VNV.

The VNV wanted Flanders to be an independent state within the German union, while *DeVlag* proclaimed unconditional loyalty to the *Führer* and the Reich – its 50,000 members were in favour of the annexation of Flanders by Germany. Naturally, Himmler supported *DeVlag*. Every leading member of *DeVlag* was obliged to join the German SS in Flanders, while members of the German SS in Flanders were ordered to join *DeVlag*, moulding the two organizations together.

In recognition of his efforts van de Wiele was promoted to SS major, thereby becoming the highest-ranking Flemish official. He enjoyed a good relationship with Léon Degrelle, the leader of the Walloons (French-speaking Belgians), to the extent that he accompanied him on public engagements. Meanwhile, van de Wiele worked enthusiastically with the Nazis, advocating the full

mobilization of the region. In 1943 he turned the entire country's youth movement over to the Hitler Youth.

On 4 December 1942, SS Second Lieutenant August Schollen, the leader of *Stormban III/1*, was shot in Brussels. His friend, First Lieutenant Robert Verbelen, the leader of *Stormban IV/1*, then began a reign of terror against the resistance and leading figures in Belgian society.

The son of a Belgian policeman, Verbelen was educated in French. He became a journalist and general secretary of the Flemish football league and he was also a member of the VNV. Although one of his brothers had joined the resistance, Verbelen was one of the first to join the *Algemeene SS Vlaanderen*. He later became leader of the Security Corps of *DeVlag*.

Once he was a member of *DeVlag*, Verbelen raised the *DeVlag-Veiligheidskorps/ DeVlag-Sicherheitskorps* in 1944, to protect its supporters. Together with the Gestapo and the SD, he cracked down on any armed resistance. As the Allies advanced into Belgium in September 1944, many members of the *Germaansche SS* fled to Germany, where they joined the *Waffen-SS*, serving with the *SS-Jagdverband 'Nordwest'*.

Shortly after that, Flanders was annexed by the Nazis and van der Wiele was appointed *Gauleiter* of the Region of Flanders. He fled to Germany to set up a government in exile.

Robert Verbelen went off to join him as part of this short-lived government, but then he moved to Austria, where he became a police informer and worked for American intelligence. In 1947 he was sentenced to death in absentia for the murder of 101 Belgian citizens. Although he was using his real name, along with a number of aliases, Verbelen was granted Austrian citizenship. However, in 1962, the Nazi-hunter Simon Wiesenthal alerted the public prosecutor in Vienna. As an Austrian citizen, Verbelen contested his extradition to Belgium so in 1965 the public prosecutor instituted proceedings against him in a Vienna court. He was charged with five counts of murder and instigation of murder. Although the Austrian jury found Verbelen guilty of instigating the murders of two people, it ruled that he had only been carrying out his superiors' orders and thus he was acquitted of committing war crimes. This acquittal was later overturned by the Austrian Supreme Court, but the case was never retried.

Verbelen continued living in Austria, where he published articles in a number of far-right publications and wrote espionage novels.

Van de Wiele enjoyed a short moment of glory, but it was all too late because the Allies had already invaded Belgium. He was tried as a traitor and sentenced to death. This punishment was later commuted to life imprisonment and he was released after 17 years. He settled in West Germany.

NORWAY

The Norwegian *Norges SS* was formed in May 1941, despite fierce opposition from Vidkun Quisling, the former defence minister who had invited Hitler to invade. Although the *Norges SS* was technically a formation within Quisling's National Union party, he had no control over it. Its leader was Norway's police chief, Jonas Lie. The *Norges SS* was backed by *Reichskommisar* Josef Terboven and Himmler flew in to administer the oath. Having sworn an oath of allegiance to both Hitler and Quisling, the new SS men were sent on a six-week induction course.

Lie was the son of a famous Norwegian literary family. He followed in the family

tradition by becoming a war correspondent during the Second World War and he later became a policeman. Even though his uncle was a passionate anti-Semite, one of his duties had been to accompany Leon Trotsky when he travelled on a freighter from Norway to Mexico in 1936. He also produced a series of detective novels under the name of Max Mauser. After leaving the National Union party in 1935 he rejoined it in 1940.

Lie became one of the first Norwegian SS volunteers in the *Waffen-SS* when he served briefly as a war correspondent in *Leibstandarte SS Adolf Hitler* during the Balkans Campaign of 1940. With him was Sverre Riisnæs, who later became Minister of Justice in the Quisling government. After forming the *Norges SS*, Lie commanded the 1st Police Company of the Norwegian Legion of the *Waffen-SS* in 1942–3, when he won the Iron Cross First Class.

Himmler mistrusted Lie, in spite of his bravery on the field, so he replaced him with Riisnæs, who was a willing servant of the Nazis. In his capacity as Minister of Justice, Riisnæs had adjusted the Norwegian legal system to legitimize the Nazis' actions and he had authorized the persecution of those who would not co-operate with the German invaders.

Lie was found dead on the day of Norway's liberation. It is thought that he had suffered a heart attack after overindulging in akvavit, a potent Norwegian drink. Riisnæs was still around, so he was arrested and charged with treason, but his mental state made him unfit to stand trial.

When war was declared on the Soviet Union in June 1941, 85 per cent of the *Norges SS*, around 130 men, joined the Norwegian SS Volunteer Legion. Five months later Quisling became president and the *Norges SS* was renamed *Germanske SS Norge* (GSN). In

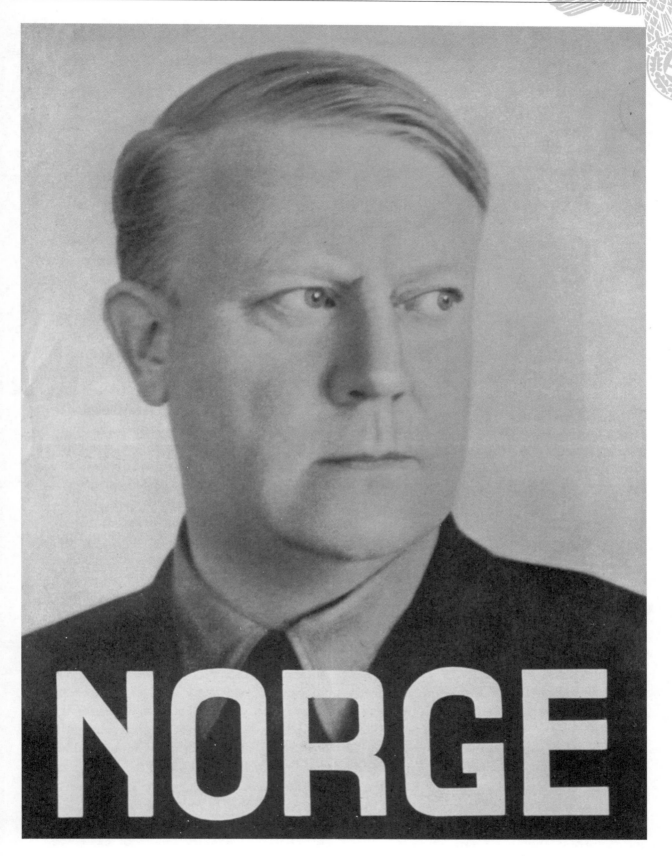

Vidkun Quisling became a puppet of the Germans after inviting Hitler to invade; he was executed as a traitor by firing squad when they left

May 1943, most Norwegian volunteers were transferred into the *SS-Panzergrenadier Norge* and soon afterwards the GSN formed a full company of its own to fight on the Eastern Front.

The total strength of the Norwegian SS in September 1944 was 1,247, with 330 at the front, 245 in the police force and 511 in emergency units. That meant that only 161 members were available to run the organization in Norway. Meanwhile, its supporters, the *Støttende Medlemmer*, numbered 3,422, while 9,137 subscribed to its newspaper, *Germaneren – Kamporgan for Germanske SS Norge*.

When Norway was liberated by the Allies in May 1945, Quisling stood trial for treason and was executed.

DENMARK

King Christian X had accepted the 'protection of the Reich' as far back as 9 April 1940, when Denmark had been threatened by aerial bombing, but the *Frikorps Danmark* only came into existence on 29 June 1941, after being formed at the instigation of the SS and the DNSAP. It is estimated that between 6,000 and 10,000 Danes served in the *Frikorps Danmark*, which saw action on the Eastern Front in 1942.

In June 1943, the *Frikorps* was disbanded and some of its men were transferred to a Danish regiment in the *SS-Freiwilligen Panzergrenadier Division Nordland*, a division

The *Germanske SS Norge* formed a full company of their own to fight on the Eastern Front

of the *Waffen-SS*. Others joined the Danish auxiliary police corps (HIPO corps) or the Schalburg Corps, a branch of the *Germanic-SS*. The Schalburg Corps was named in honour of the former leader of the *Frikorps*, Christian Frederik von Schalburg, who had been killed in action on 2 June 1942. Unlike the *Germanic-SS* units in Norway and the Netherlands, this particular detachment was not a part of the local Nazi party. Instead it was a separate organization, whose leader was Knud Børge Martinsen.

After joining the Danish army in 1928, Martinsen was on the general staff when Germany occupied Denmark in 1940. Two weeks later, he joined the National Socialist Workers' Party of Denmark (DNSAP). He then resigned in order to join the *Waffen-SS*, serving with *Frikorps Danmark* under Christian Frederik von Schalburg. After Schalburg's death, Martinsen took command of the *Frikorps*. When it was disbanded, he was transferred to the *SS-Freiwilligen Panzergrenadier Division Nordland*.

After two months, Martinsen returned to Denmark to take command of the Schalburg Corps, which had become a recruitment unit for the *Waffen-SS*. In October 1944, he was arrested by the Gestapo and imprisoned in Berlin. He eventually escaped and made his way back to Denmark, where he was arrested. After a trial he was sentenced to death and executed by firing squad in Copenhagen.

Members of the Schalburg Corps who had not had any combat experience on the Eastern Front had to endure six weeks of political indoctrination and combat training. The corps was divided into two groups: one consisted of regular soldiers and the other, the Danish People's Defence, was made up of civilians. Some of them were expected to provide financial backing. Members of the corps were used as a guard battalion to protect railroads and crossroads from sabotage.

In July 1944, the Schalburg Corps was incorporated into the SS as the SS Training Battalion Schalburg, first under SS Major Poul Neergaard-Jacobsen and then under SS First Lieutenant Egill Poulsen. After six months, it was renamed the SS Guard Battalion Zealand. It was officially disbanded on 28 February 1945.

FRANCE

While the French had the *Légion des Volontaires Français* (LVF), they did not have an *SS-Allgemeine* group. However, the SS formed close links with Vichy France's paramilitary *Milice* (Militia), whose job it was to round up the Jews and summarily execute members of the resistance. The force later merged with the LVF to form the *SS-Charlemagne Division*. Few were prosecuted after the war.

SWITZERLAND

There was even support for the Nazis in neutral Switzerland. That is, if Switzerland merited the description. The Germans had the power to flatten Switzerland whenever they chose, but with so many factories churning out precision components, not to mention the fact that Switzerland was a ready market for Nazi gold, the 'neutral' arrangement suited both sides very well.

Swiss doctor Franz Riedweg was one of the Nazi Party's most ardent Swiss supporters. After studying medicine in Berne, Rostock and Berlin, he became a member of the Swiss National Front. In 1936, he became a political adviser to Jean-Marie Musy, a member of the Federal Council of Switzerland, and a year later he joined the ranks of Action Against Communism, which produced the propaganda film *The Red Plague*.

His next move was to marry the daughter of war minister Werner von Blomberg, which he did in 1938. It was a good tactic for a would-be Nazi, because he was soon rubbing shoulders with Goebbels, Himmler and Heydrich. No wonder he was seen as the most influential Swiss citizen in Nazi Germany during the Second World War. He was then made a lieutenant colonel in the SS, which propelled him into the *Leibstandarte SS Adolf Hitler*, where he served as a doctor during the invasion of Poland, before going to France.

In 1941, he became the medical officer of the *SS-Hauptamt* in Berlin and in the same year he started the 'Panorama House' in Stuttgart, which served as a detention centre for Swiss nationals. He also became the director of non-German volunteers to the *Waffen-SS*. A couple of years later he headed the Germanic control centre in the SS headquarters and was awarded the Iron Cross. A year after that, in 1944, he received orders to form the *Schweizer Sportbund*, or the *Germanische SS Schweiz*, but the war was nearing its end and the Swiss SS was never formed. The Swiss then withdrew his citizenship.

Undaunted, he went off to war with *III Germanisches Panzer Korps*, but he was captured in Mecklenburg-Vorpommem. In his absence, he was tried by a Swiss court for attempting to destroy the independence of Switzerland by military means and was sentenced to 16 years' imprisonment. However, he continued working as a doctor in Munich, where he died at the age of 98. His way of life had obviously suited him.

Policing the SS

The SS was a law unto itself. After three top SS men at Dachau concentration camp had been charged with incitement to murder in 1934, Himmler decided that it would be a good idea to place the SS above German law and make it answerable only to the *Hauptamt SS Gericht* (Head Office SS Court). Led by SS Lieutenant-Colonel Franz Breihaupt, some 600 lawyers investigated and prosecuted cases against people who had been charged with violating the SS code of honour, though Himmler often intervened and altered the sentences. By 1944, there were 12 offices throughout Germany and 38 courts across the Reich.

After winning an Iron Cross in the First World War, Breihaupt joined the Nazi Party in 1931 and the SS in the following year. In 1933, he was elected to the Reichstag, serving on Himmler's staff from 1934 onwards. Rising effortlessly through the ranks, he had become an SS lieutenant-general by the time he took over the *Hauptamt SS Gericht*. He died on 28 April 1945, apparently murdered by his aide, SS Second Lieutenant Karl Lang.

While the *Hauptamt SS Gericht* was intended to be a convenient way of making SS members immune to prosecution in the ordinary course of events, some of its staff took their jobs seriously. Too seriously for some. One of them was SS First Lieutenant Konrad Morgen, who became known as the 'Bloodhound Judge'. Morgen was regarded as a pacifist, even more so when he published *War Propaganda and the Prevention of War* in 1936. As a lawyer, his belief in the primacy of law in Hitler's increasingly dictatorial regime had brought him into conflict with a provincial magistrate. In order to save

his career, he had accepted a post as an assistant judge with the *Hauptamt SS Gericht*. When he was posted to Krakow, he began investigating cases of corruption, but his scrupulous regard for the law irritated the police chief, SS Lieutenant-General Friedrich Krüger. As a punishment, he was sent to join the *SS-Wiking* Division, which was stationed on the Eastern Front at the time.

Morgen should have expected that sort of treatment at the hands of Krüger. The son of a military family, Krüger served as an officer during the First World War, when he was wounded three times and won the Iron Cross First and Second Class. After serving in the *Freikorps*, he joined the Nazi Party in 1929 and the SS in 1931, but after two months he quit to join the SA, where he served on Röhm's personal staff. He was spared on the Night of the Long Knives because his switch to the SA was seen as a purely pragmatic move. After Röhm's death he switched back to the SS again.

In October 1939, he was appointed High SS and police leader in occupied Poland. As such, he was responsible for crushing rebellions in the extermination camps. He was obviously unpopular because two bombs were thrown at his car at one point, though he survived. However, he was dismissed in November 1943 after falling out with the governor-general, Hans Frank.

He was then sent off to Nazi-occupied Yugoslavia with the 7th SS Mountain Infantry 'Prince Eugen' Division, where he fought with the partisans.

His unit became infamous for its civilian atrocities. After going on to fight in Finland he committed suicide in Austria in May 1945. Hitler was already dead by then.

His older brother was SS Lieutenant-General Walter Krüger (1890–1945), who formed the

Karl Otto Koch (seen above with his wife Ilse, their dog and son) killed the doctor who had treated him for syphilis so the secret never got out

SS-Standarte Germania and took part in the siege of Leningrad, among other things. Like his brother, he committed suicide at the end of the war. There was nothing left to live for now the Nazi dream was shattered.

Although Friedrich Krüger had sent Morgen off to the Eastern Front, the lawyer's investigative skills were seen as a more valuable asset than his fighting abilities, so he was dragged back and posted to the SS Criminal Police Division (RKPA), where he would deal with financial crimes.

Running an eye over the death list for Buchenwald concentration camp, the Higher SS and police leader for Weimar, SS Lieutenant-General Josias, Prince of Waldeck and Pyrmont,

stopped short when he reached the name of Dr Walter Krämmer, who had once treated him. Investigating, Josias discovered that the camp commandant, SS Colonel Karl Otto Koch, had killed Krämmer and a medical orderly named Karl Peixof because they had treated him for syphilis, something that Koch wanted covered up. Another prisoner had been 'shot while trying to escape' when he had been sent to fetch water some distance from the camp. Josias asked Morgen to investigate.

Perhaps the grandest member of the SS, Josias was a cousin of Queen Wilhelmina of the Netherlands and a relative of the British royal family. He was born in the family castle at Bad Arolsen. After being injured in the First

World War, he joined the Nazi Party in 1929 and the SS in the following year. Elected as the Reichstag member for Düsseldorf-West in 1933, he was promoted to the rank of SS lieutenant-general. In 1939, he became the Higher SS and police leader for Weimar and consequently had authority over Buchenwald concentration camp which was situated nearby.

Two years later he was promoted to the position of high commissioner of police in occupied France. One of his first acts was to announce that French hostages would be placed on German troop trains in order to discourage sabotage attempts on them. He was made a full general in the *Waffen-SS* in July 1944. Arrested on 13 April 1945, he was accused of overseeing Buchenwald and being involved in the execution of Karl Otto Koch. Found guilty, he was sentenced to life imprisonment in the very camp that he claimed to know little about. His sentence was commuted to twenty years but he was released after just three years, on medical grounds.

Morgen was already investigating another case at Buchenwald at the time. Working in collusion with Koch, a Nazi provisions merchant named Bornschein had been profiteering while supplying the camp. In order to avoid prosecution by the local police, Bornschein had joined the *Waffen-SS*, so only the RKPA had jurisdiction. Morgen moved into the Hotel Elephant in Weimar, one of Hitler's favourite hostelries. After prosecuting Bornschein, Morgen amassed evidence showing that Koch had been hiring out camp labourers to civilians, racketeering in food supplies, murdering unco-operative inmates and generally running the camp for his own profit.

By this time Koch had been moved to Majdanek concentration camp in Lublin, eastern Poland, but his wife, Ilse, was still

The unmistakably patrician air of Prince Josias zu Waldeck-Pyrmont: Buchenwald fell under his jurisdiction

'The Singing Forest' at Buchenwald, where inmates were hung from trees, was a favourite haunt of sadistic SS officer Martin Sommer

living at the commandant's house in Buchenwald. Morgen intercepted the couple's letters and examined their bank accounts. It was like lifting the lid from a can of worms. He soon discovered that Koch had embezzled at least 100,000 marks and he also found proof of the murders of Dr Krämmer and Karl Peixof. It appeared that witnesses to the murders had been slain as well, while camp officials such as Dr Waldemar Houst, the camp doctor, were also involved in the murders and in acts of sadism.

Josias filed charges of incitement to murder against Koch, and Morgen added allegations of embezzlement. He also arraigned other members of the camp staff. The charges were passed to the chief of the criminal police, SS Major-General Artur Nebe, who relayed them to Gestapo chief SS Major-General Heinrich Müller. Next they went to Ernst Kaltenbrunner, head of the RSHA. The chief of the SS legal department took one look at the charges and passed them on to Himmler. Fearing that the file may be overlooked or ignored, Morgen sent a carefully worded telegram to Himmler outlining the case. Himmler was ever anxious that nothing should besmirch the honour of the SS – except mass murder, of course – so he gave Morgen full authority to proceed against Koch.

After winning the Iron Cross Second Class, Koch was captured by the British on the Western Front, returning to Germany in 1919. In 1931, he joined the Nazi Party and the SS and four years later he became commandant of Columbia-Haus concentration camp in Berlin-Tempelhof, before taking over at

Sachsenhausen in 1937. He moved to Buchen-wald in 1941 and was then transferred to Majdanek following allegations of corruption, fraud, embezzlement, drunkenness, sexual offences and murder.

After a year, he was relieved of duty when 86 Soviet prisoners of war escaped. Accused of criminal negligence, he was returned to Berlin, where he faced the charges drawn up by Josias, Prince of Waldeck and Pyrmont, and Konrad Morgen. At his trial, Koch was sentenced to death for disgracing both himself and the SS. He was executed by firing squad on 5 April 1945, one week before American troops arrived to liberate the camp.

Koch was certainly a criminal of the first order, yet the dual standards of the SS were such that someone like Nebe, who had arguably committed even greater crimes, could be the police chief who first brought him to justice. Nebe had walked a curious tightrope during his SS career. He was often appalled by the atrocities he was asked to commit, yet he went along with them just the same. He was involved in several plots against Hitler and others, but he experimented with a new method for gassing Jews.

Gassed twice himself in the First World War, Nebe joined the criminal police (Kripo) in 1920. By 1924, he had become a commissioner. In 1931, he joined the Nazi Party and the SS on the same day.

Then came his first killing. In 1933, Rudolf

Artur Nebe was often appalled by the atrocities he was asked to commit, yet he went along with them all the same

Diels, then head of the Gestapo, ordered Nebe to dispose of Gregor Strasser. After that, various reorganizations of the police force resulted in Nebe becoming head of the national criminal police under the RSHA, reporting directly to Heydrich. He regularly dined with Heydrich and Himmler.

In order to test Nebe's loyalty, Himmler gave him command of *Einsatzgruppe B*. Nebe was so appalled by Heydrich's murderous orders that he reported them to the group surrounding Colonel Hans Oster, who opposed Hitler's war aims. Trying to wriggle out of the job, Nebe asked to be made head of the International Police Commission, but Oster and some others persuaded him to take the *Einsatzgruppe* job so that he could give them up-to-date information from inside the SS and the Gestapo. Nebe's group killed 46,000 people but that was only a fraction of the 221,000 murders that had been racked up by *Einsatzgruppe A*, which was led by SS Major-General Franz-Walter Stahlecker. Stahlecker was killed by Soviet partisans in March 1942.

Nebe was sickened by the murders but he found himself on the verge of a nervous breakdown when his driver killed himself over what he had witnessed. Nevertheless, Himmler ordered him to arrange the execution of 100 Jews during his visit to Minsk. As if killing innocent people were not enough, Nebe was

Implicated in the plot to kill Hitler in 1944, Artur Nebe was hanged from a meat hook with piano wire by order of the *Führer*

ordered to have sex with two of his female victims. This was the execution at which Himmler nearly fainted because someone's brains splattered on his coat. Afterwards Nebe was ordered to find a method of killing that would not be so distressing for the executioners. He experimented with gassing his victims by pumping the exhaust gases from a truck into the sealed rear compartment.

After the war, movie footage of his hideous research was found in his Berlin apartment.

Yet Nebe still appeared to see himself as a concerned observer. When he attended the Wannsee Conference in 1942 he leaked the details of the 'Final Solution' to Hans Oster, his fellow conspirator. However, he did not demur when Gestapo chief Heinrich Müller ordered him to select 50 out of the 73 recaptured prisoners for execution after the 'Great Escape' from Stalag Luft III in March 1944. He always did what was asked of him.

Nebe's involvement in several plots against the Nazi hierarchy proved to be his final undoing. He was involved in a 1938 plot to overthrow Hitler, for instance, and he also conspired to ruin Himmler's attempt to smear General Werner von Fritsch. All of that apparently escaped detection, but his association with the 'Valkyrie' plot to kill Hitler on 20 July 1944 did not pass unnoticed. He was supposed to have led a team of 12 policemen to kill Himmler, but the message never reached him. Nevertheless, he went into hiding, but he was betrayed by a girlfriend. Sentenced to death by the *Volksgerichtshof* (People's Court), he was hanged.

Heinrich Müller was far less complicated than Nebe. He despised Hitler and yet he rounded up those who plotted against him, because that was his job.

After serving as a pilot in the First World War and winning the Iron Cross, Müller witnessed the shooting of hostages in the short-lived Bavarian Soviet Republic, which was said to have given him a lifelong hatred of communism. Then in 1919 he joined the political department of the Bavarian police force. In 1931 he was the investigating officer when Hitler's niece, Geli Raubal, was shot, and it was said that he took a bribe to ensure the scandal would not taint Hitler, who was

From the left: Franz Ziereis, Ernst Kaltenbrunner and Himmler, among others, inspect Mauthausen KZ, April 1941

thought to have killed Geli in a fit of jealousy.

A bribe sounds about right. He would not have been motivated by goodwill, because he once referred to Hitler as 'an immigrant unemployed house painter' and 'an Austrian draft-dodger'. Perhaps that is why he did not become a member of the Nazi Party until 1939. Nevertheless, Heydrich chose him to replace Diels as head of the Gestapo, because Diels was Göring's man. Müller became Adolf Eichmann's boss and he also received reports on the operations of the *Einsatzgruppen*. Eichmann ran the Gestapo's Office of Resettlement and then its Office of Jewish Affairs.

After the 20 July plot, Müller was in charge of the investigating committee that rounded up the conspirators. He was awarded the Knight's Cross for his efforts. Then on 29 April 1945, with the Red Army fighting its way into Berlin, Müller was put in charge of the interrogation and execution of Hermann Fegelein, who was Himmler's liaison officer with Hitler and Eva Braun's brother-in-law. Himmler had tried to negotiate with the Western Allies. Two days later

Müller disappeared to no one knows where.

Like Müller, Kaltenbrunner was a man who did his duty. He made sure that nothing stood in the way of the German nation, no matter what the human cost.

Born in Ried im Innkreis, Austria, not far from Braunau am Inn, Hitler's birthplace, Kaltenbrunner studied law at the University of Graz. He acquired a deep scar on his face during his student days, which he attributed to duelling, though some said it was caused by a drink-related car accident.

In 1932 he joined the Nazi Party in Austria and then he formed an *SS-Sturmbann* with Adolf Eichmann. Following the murder of Engelbert Dollfuss, he was jailed for six months for conspiracy. As leader of the Austrian SS, he assisted in the *Anschluss*, was promoted to SS major-general and became a member of the Reichstag in 1938.

After Heydrich's death, Kaltenbrunner was appointed as his successor – when Himmler had done the job himself for eight months – even though Himmler complained of his drinking. Kaltenbrunner headed Operation Long Jump, a failed attempt to assassinate Churchill, Roosevelt and Stalin at their meeting in Tehran in 1943 and he was awarded the Knight's Cross after preparing the case against *Abwehr* chief Wilhelm Canaris, following the 20 July plot. As the war drew to a close, he moved his headquarters to Altaussee in Austria, the so-called 'Alpine redoubt' where hardliners aimed to continue the war.

At Nuremberg, Kaltenbrunner was found guilty of war crimes and crimes against humanity and was sentenced to death. He went to the gallows denying he knew anything of the crimes of which he was accused. The three children he had with his wife, and the two he had with his mistress, all survived the war.

Morgen takes on Himmler

While investigating Koch, Morgen began to look into what was happening at Majdanek. In early November 1943, he became an accidental eyewitness to part of Operation Harvest Festival – the liquidation of three large and several smaller Jewish labour camps in the Lublin district of eastern Poland and the murder of their 50,000 inmates. At the Poniatowa labour camp Morgen watched as more than 15,000 inmates of all ages and both sexes reported to the execution site, where they handed over their personal effects and clothing and then went naked into the trenches, where they were shot. But as all of this had been personally authorized by Himmler, there was nothing Morgen could do about it.

Camp Commandant *SS-Oberführer* Christian Wirth gave Morgen a tour of the extermination camps at Treblinka, Sobibor and Belzec, where he saw the gas chambers, the crematoria and the mass graves. Believing this to be evidence of localized crime, he began to investigate.

Then he discovered that the orders for the mass murders at these camps had come directly from Hitler's chancellery and could not be stopped by the SS legal department. However, he began to prosecute individual SS officers for the 'arbitrary killings' that took place outside the directives of the 'Final Solution'. He also investigated cases of cruelty, corruption and other comparatively minor crimes. Eventually Himmler had to tell him to back off.

Christian Wirth was a former Stuttgart policeman who had been recommended to Himmler by Nebe. He headed the T-4 Euthanasia Programme that eliminated disabled people and mental patients, as well as others who were considered incurable, and he also oversaw mass sterilization projects.

Franz Stangl, the commandant of the Sobibor and Treblinka death camps, described Wirth as

a gross and florid man … When he spoke about the necessity of this euthanasia operation, he wasn't speaking in humane or scientific terms, the way Dr Werner at T-4 had described it to me. He laughed. He spoke of 'doing away with useless mouths', and that 'sentimental slobber' about such people made him 'puke'.

Born in Austria, Stangl joined the police force and became a member of the Nazi Party in 1931, when it was illegal. After the *Anschluss*, he was promoted quickly up the ranks. Himmler appointed him superintendent of the T-4 Programme at the Euthanasia Institute at Schloss Hartheim. It was there that he first met Christian Wirth, who was later involved in gassing Jews at Chelmno and Belzec.

In 1942, he was transferred to Poland where he worked under Odilo Globocnik (see Chapter Seven) and he became the commandant of

Sachsenhausen concentration camp, 22 miles (35km) from Berlin, was established in 1938 and initially used to house political prisoners

Sobibor extermination camp. Around 10,000 Jews were killed before Stangl became the commandant of Treblinka.

'I remember Wirth standing there, next to the pits full of black-blue corpses,' said Stangl. 'Wirth said: "What shall we do with rotting garbage?" I think unconsciously that started me thinking of them as cargo' – which is what Stangl began calling his victims.

Stangl oversaw the murder of 700,000 people at Treblinka. The camp was second only to Auschwitz in the numbers that were gassed. During this barbarous operation, the victims were robbed of large amounts of money in different currencies – £400,000, $2,800,000 and 12,000,000 roubles – as well as 145 kilograms

of gold from rings and teeth and 4,000 carats of diamonds. The criminals even took hair, clothing and spectacles.

As the Red Army advanced the camp was destroyed, leaving only 40 surviving inmates. The guards were sent to fight the Yugoslav partisans, which was a virtual death sentence. Stangl was arrested after the war, but he escaped to Brazil where he worked in the Volkswagen factory in São Paulo under his own name. Howesver, a disaffected relative reported his whereabouts to Simon Wiesenthal and in 1969 he was extradited to Germany, where he stood trial for the murder of around 900,000 people.

He admitted to these killings but like a true

grass was trimmed and a sign was hung over the gate, saying: 'Entrance to the Jewish state.' Over the entrance to the gas chamber itself hung a banner made from a synagogue curtain which said, in Hebrew: 'This is the gate of the Lord into which the righteous shall enter.'

After killing 1.7 million Polish Jews and thousands of gypsies, Wirth was transferred to San Sabba concentration camp in Trieste where he was also responsible for suppressing the partisans in occupied Yugoslavia. Those who had been on the extermination programme often found themselves being given dangerous assignments to get rid of them. Wirth was killed by partisans in May 1944, while travelling in an open-topped car.

In 1944, Morgen began investigating the commandant of Auschwitz extermination camp, Rudolf Höss. Needless to say, his enquiries were not welcomed. One of Morgen's aides, SS Battalion Sergeant Major Gerhard Putsch, vanished without a trace and the hut where Morgen kept his files was burnt to the ground. However, he managed to prosecute several high-ranking Nazis such as Maximilian Grabner, the Gestapo chief and head torturer at Auschwitz, who was arraigned for theft and corruption, and the commandant of Dachau, Alex Piorkowski, who was also convicted of corruption. Koch's successor at Majdanek, Hermann Florstedt, was another criminal who was successfully put on trial. He was executed by the SS for corruption and arbitrary killing on 15 April 1945.

Like many SS monsters, the character and behaviour of Rudolf Höss is riddled with paradox. As a child he had hoped to become a Catholic priest and during the First World War he became the youngest NCO to serve in the German army. He was wounded several times and he won the Iron Cross. After the war he joined the *Freikorps*, then in 1922 he renounced

psychopath he said: 'My conscience is clear. I was simply doing my duty.'

He was sentenced to life imprisonment and he died in jail.

Because of opposition from the Church, T-4 was cancelled and Wirth was transferred to Poland to oversee the gassing of the gypsies and the Jews. He had no time for the mobile units being used at Chelmno extermination camp. At Belzec, Sobibor and Treblinka he constructed three special 'shower rooms', believing that the victims would be pacified by the idea that they were going to have a shower, though an eyewitness recalled Wirth striking a hesitating woman across the face with the whip he always carried. Exhaust gas from a diesel engine was then pumped in through the shower heads. Geraniums were planted outside, the his Catholic faith and joined the Nazi Party. In the following year Höss and Martin Bormann, later Hitler's private secretary, were sentenced to life imprisonment for the murder of school-teacher Walter Kadow, whom they suspected of reporting *Freikorps* members to the French authorities in the occupied Ruhr.

Released in 1928 as part of a general amnesty, Höss joined the Artaman League, which promoted a clean-living, rural lifestyle. In 1929 he married Hedwig Hensel, who bore him five children, then in 1934 he joined the *SS-Totenkopfverbände*. He served as an administrator at Dachau for four years. According to his autobiography, he was squeamish about the corporal punishment that was inflicted on the inmates but he was unconcerned when he witnessed executions.

After a period at Sachsenhausen he became the first commandant of Auschwitz, which was then only a detention camp. However, he greatly expanded its facilities. In June 1941 he received orders that Hitler had decreed the physical extermination of all European Jews, which would take place at Auschwitz. Höss's camp had been chosen because it had good rail links and it was isolated, so it would be easier to maintain secrecy. The only person he told was his wife, who lived at the camp with their children. After he told her, she was reluctant to sleep with him. It is said that he then had an affair with an inmate, who was disposed of by being sent to the gas chamber. A complex man, he also appears to have written poetry about the beauty of the place.

Following a fact-finding visit to Treblinka, Höss decided that he could do better. Treblinka's gas chambers only accommodated 200 people, but Höss made his chambers ten times larger, so that they had a capacity of 2,000. Engine exhaust fumes were used to murder

the inmates at Treblinka, but that did not look very efficient to Höss, so he experimented with sulphuric acid and then with Zyklon B. This was quicker, taking between 3 and 15 minutes – 'We knew when the people were dead because they stopped screaming,' he said.

Höss prided himself on his ability to conceal the truth from his victims. He thought that they would go willingly into the gas chambers if they were told that they were going to be deloused. The only problem was that the crematoria could not keep up with the number of bodies coming out of the gas chambers. Consequently some of the bodies had to be burnt in pits, so the victims were alerted by the reek of burning flesh.

Höss claimed to have worried about murdering children – all children were sent to the gas chambers because they were of no use as forced labour. But Eichmann assured him that if the children were killed first there would not be a new generation to wreak revenge on them. Despite his professed concern, Höss had no qualms about the hideous experiments that the doctors were performing on inmates, nor did he care that the Gestapo were torturing some of the prisoners. Promoted to the position of deputy inspector of concentration camps in December 1943, Höss returned to Auschwitz to oversee the murder of 430,000 Hungarian Jews in May 1944. In the last days of the war he fled ahead of the Red Army and hid in Germany under the name of Fritz Lang. He might well have remained anonymous, but his wife gave him away. She could not come to terms with the fact that she had married a monster. After appearing at Nuremberg as a witness, he was handed over to the Polish authorities.

At his trial he was accused of murdering three-and-a-half million people.

'No. Only two-and-a-half million,' Höss

replied. 'The rest died from disease and starvation.'

Sentenced to death, he was hanged at Auschwitz, on the very gallows he had constructed himself.

If he was to have any chance of stopping the Holocaust, Morgen knew that he would have to take the matter up with Himmler himself. He arranged a meeting, but Himmler cancelled the appointment at the last minute. Morgen was preparing a full investigation of Auschwitz when he received direct orders from Hitler's office commanding him to cease his activities. Nevertheless, he brought 800 cases of corruption and obtained at least 200 convictions. It is also thought that he was at least partly responsible for the closure of the extermination camps at Treblinka, Sobibor and Belzec in 1943 and 1944.

After the war, the Allies made use of the evidence Morgen had amassed when they prosecuted the Nazi war criminals and he appeared as a witness for the prosecution in several cases. Grabner and Piorkowski were hanged as a result. However, he refused to testify against Ilse Koch because he did not have any concrete proof that she had committed any of the crimes that she was charged with – though he did believe that she was guilty. Attempts were made by the Allied authorities to intimidate him – he was even threatened with extradition to the Soviet Union. But this was a man who had stood up

The wife of Höss gave him away. She could not come to terms with the fact that she had married a monster

to the Nazis. Eventually, they let him go. He continued practising law in West Germany, where he died in 1976.

Morgen might not have been sure of Ilse Koch's guilt, but many others were. Known as the 'Witch of Buchenwald' – or sometimes the 'Bitch of Buchenwald' – she met the camp's commandant, Karl Otto Koch, when he was a guard at Sachsenhausen. It was alleged that she sadistically tortured inmates and forced them to rape one another for her own amusement.

Arrested alongside her husband for murder and embezzlement, she was acquitted by an SS court, but in June 1945 she was arrested by the Americans. It was alleged that she had ordered the murder of certain people so that she could have their tattooed skin made into lampshades. However, Konrad Morgen could find no evidence for this story. Nevertheless, she was found guilty of aiding and abetting her husband and participating in some of the murders at Buchenwald. She was sentenced to life imprisonment. Released after two years by the military governor of the American zone of occupation in Germany, she was arrested again. This time she stood trial before a West German court for the instigation of some 135 murders. Sentenced to life imprisonment again, she hanged herself in prison.

Despite Konrad Morgen's efforts, around six million Jews would lose their lives in the Nazi camps.

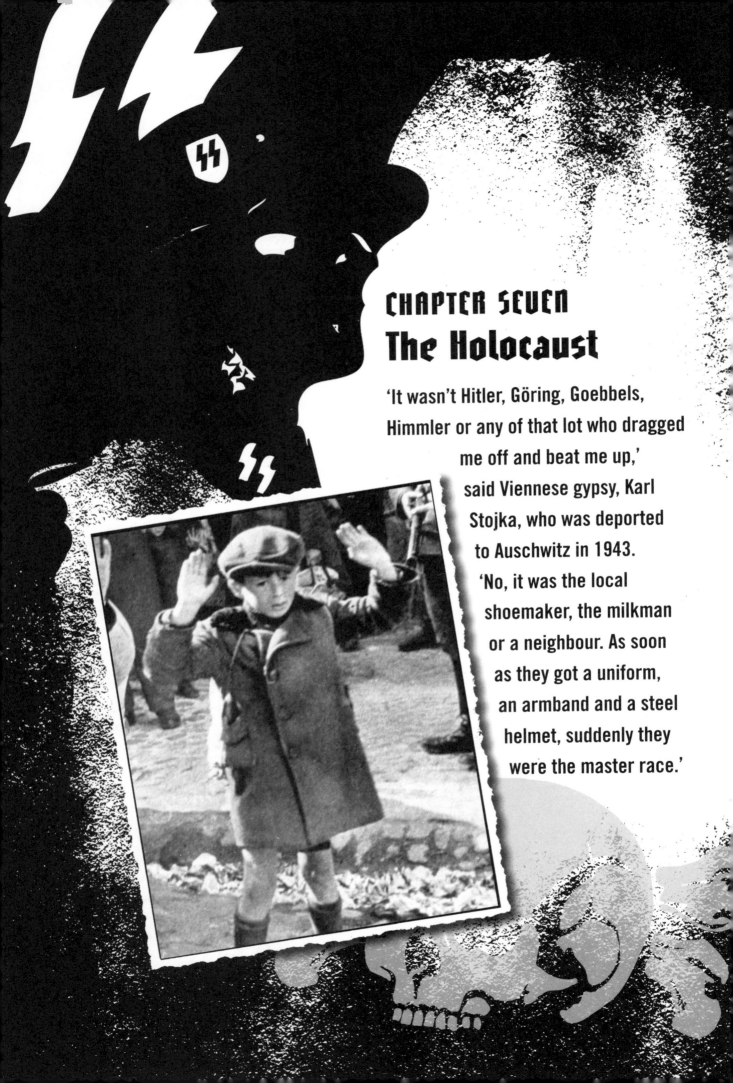

CHAPTER SEVEN
The Holocaust

'It wasn't Hitler, Göring, Goebbels, Himmler or any of that lot who dragged me off and beat me up,' said Viennese gypsy, Karl Stojka, who was deported to Auschwitz in 1943. 'No, it was the local shoemaker, the milkman or a neighbour. As soon as they got a uniform, an armband and a steel helmet, suddenly they were the master race.'

I N 1922, JOURNALIST Joseph Hell asked Hitler what he would do about the Jews. After falling into 'a kind of paroxysm', Hitler gradually worked himself up into a frenzy.

Once I really am in power, my first and foremost task will be the annihilation of the Jews. As soon as I have the power to do so, I will have gallows built in rows – at the Marienplatz in Munich, for example – as many as traffic allows. Then the Jews will be hanged indiscriminately, and they will remain hanging until they stink; they will hang there as long as the principles of hygiene permit. As soon as they have been untied, the next batch will be strung up, and so on down the line, until the last Jew in Munich has been exterminated. Other cities will follow suit, precisely in this fashion, until all Germany has been completely cleansed of Jews.

These views were reiterated in *Mein Kampf*, published in 1926:

The personification of the devil as the symbol of all evil assumes the living shape of the Jew … by defending myself against the Jew, I am fighting for the work of the Lord.

As Hitler's most loyal disciple, Heinrich Himmler also spoke venomously about the 'extermination' of the Jews. So far it had all been talk, but the Enabling Act of 23 March 1933 changed everything. The Nazis could now pass laws without recourse to the Reichstag. Just over a week later, on 1 April 1933, a boycott of Jewish businesses began. Jewish shops and professional offices were encircled by SA troops, who attempted to deter potential clients with words and posters. Anti-Semitic slogans were scrawled or painted on some of the buildings.

Then on 7 April the Law of the Restoration of the Professional Civil Service was passed, which prevented Jews from working for the state. Other laws restricted the number of Jewish students in German schools and universities, prohibited Jews from owning farms and forbade 'Jewish activities' in the medical and legal professions. In other words, Jews were having their livelihoods taken from them.

Things soon got worse. Hitler declared that anyone who was considered to be an 'enemy of the state', or a communist, could be arrested and imprisoned without trial. Himmler's bully-boys were then turned loose into the streets, where they wrought havoc amongst the terrified citizens. Dachau, the first concentration camp in Germany, had been opened in March 1933 and thousands of innocent detainees soon began to pour through its gates. Other camps quickly followed. It was not long before the political prisoners under Himmler's control could be counted in millions.

In 1935, the Nuremberg Laws prevented Jews from marrying non-Jews, annulled existing marriages and deprived Jews of citizenship and civil rights. If these laws did not solve the 'Jewish problem', Hitler told the Reichstag, it 'must then be handed over by law to the National Socialist Party for a final solution'.

Many Jews had already left Germany. After being told that the Berlin Philharmonic's concert hall would be burnt down if he did not stop conducting, Bruno Walter fled to Austria. He took French citizenship in 1938 and headed to the United States in 1939, which would become his permanent home. The conductor and composer Otto Klemperer followed suit by heading for Los Angeles, while playwright Bertolt Brecht went to Scandinavia in 1933 and then moved on to the United States. Albert

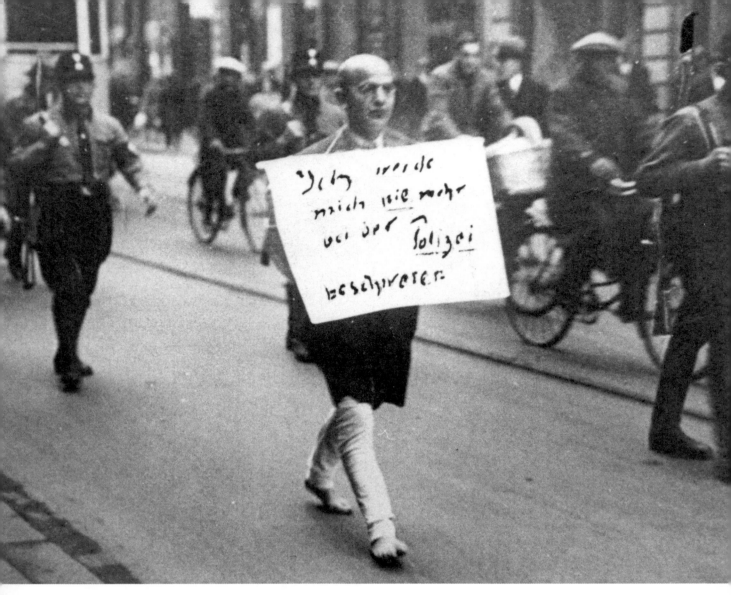

'I will never again complain to the police' – Nazi thugs taunt Munich lawyer Michael Siegel, 1933. He survived and died in Peru at the age of 97

Einstein renounced his German citizenship and found a home in Princeton. Nazi stormtroopers retaliated by ransacking his summer home at Caputh, near Berlin, and confiscating his yacht. Following the *Anschluss*, Sigmund Freud left Austria for England, where he died the following year.

In Hanover, a young Polish Jew named Herschel Grynszpan had suffered persecution at school, so he decided to emigrate to Palestine. When he was told that he would have to wait for a year, he went to Paris. He entered France illegally because he had no means of support – Jews were not permitted to take money out of Germany at that time. Unable to work, he fell on hard times. Meanwhile his parents were begging him for help. The Germans had stripped 12,000 Polish Jews of their property and deported

them to Poland, but the Polish authorities had revoked their citizenship and refused them entry. Overnight they had become stateless refugees. By 7 November 1938 Grynszpan could not take any more so he bought a gun and walked to the German embassy, where he shot junior official Ernst vom Rath. He claimed that he was acting on behalf of 12,000 persecuted Jews. Vom Rath died on 9 November, the 15th anniversary of the Beer Hall Putsch. Grynszpan's action had provided the very excuse that the Nazis had been looking for.

Goebbels made an inflammatory speech, urging 'spontaneous demonstrations' against the Jews. Telephone orders then went out, after which the SS joined the SA on the streets of Germany and Austria. The gleeful troops indulged themselves in an orgy of destruction.

More than 7,000 Jewish shops were smashed up and looted in what became known as *Kristallnacht* (Night of Broken Glass). Jewish homes, hospitals, schools and cemeteries were attacked and more than 1,000 synagogues were burnt down or otherwise vandalized. The official death toll was 91, but it is thought that many more people died in the attacks. In Berlin, fashionably dressed women clapped and laughed to see the Jews being savagely beaten by youths armed with lead piping. Some even held their babies up high, so they could witness the spectacle. The cost of broken windows alone came to millions of Reichsmarks. When Göring heard that the broken glass would have to be replaced by imported glass, bought with scarce foreign currency, he said: 'They should have killed more Jews and broken less glass.'

Some 30,000 Jewish men between the ages of 16 and 60 were arrested and handed over to the SS. The concentration camps at Dachau, Buchenwald and Sachsenhausen were expanded to meet the demand. Inmates were only released if they could show that they intended to emigrate, leaving behind whatever wealth they had. The Jews were forced to clear the rubble from their destroyed synagogues and the proceeds of any insurance claims were confiscated. On top of that, the Nazi government imposed a fine on the Jewish community of one billion Reichsmarks – around £100 million or $400 million in 1938. Jewish children were forbidden to go to school from 15 November onwards and the local authorities imposed curfews. By December, Jews were barred from theatres and other public places. They had to travel in separate compartments in railway trains and their property was seized as part of a programme of 'Aryanization'.

Those who had been delivered into the hands of the SS could expect no mercy.

The morning after: a Jewish business in Magdeburg in the aftermath of *Kristallnacht*, November 1938

'Forget your wives and children,' one SS camp commandant told the new arrivals. 'Here you will die like dogs.'

And die they did. They died because of the insanitary conditions, the starvation rations and the heavy work. Prisoners worked at least eleven hours a day, six days a week and punishments were brutal. Inmates would be subjected to 25 lashes for stealing a cigarette and the punishment for being late for roll-call was a long period in solitary confinement. Some victims went insane. Anyone who talked politics was summarily executed.

Between 1933 and 1939, Hitler occasionally issued broad amnesties. Those who were released were forced to sign affidavits which declared that they had been well treated. But for many the only release was death. SS guards were ordered to shoot anyone who tried to escape, refused to obey an order or was guilty of any form of mutiny. Guards were told: 'Any pity whatever for the enemies of the state is unworthy of an SS man.'

At first, releases and fresh arrests were kept more or less in balance, so the prison population hovered around the 25,000 mark. However, the *Anschluss* and the occupation of Czechoslovakia resulted in a further 75,000 arrests. More victims would be rounded up in Poland and the other occupied territories.

And many German citizens were arrested too. In October 1941 alone, 15,160 ordinary people were detained by the Gestapo. Some were thought to be hindering the war effort, while others had just been grumbling about it. With all of these seizures the number of concentration camp inmates climbed to 220,000. Some camps were so overcrowded that a fifth of the prisoners died every six months. The slogan *Arbeit Macht Frei* ('work will make you free') was placed at the entrances to a number of camps. It can only have been meant as a cruel insult.

As well as Jews, the camps were occupied by trade unionists and Social Democrats –

A workers' detail returns to Sachsenhausen concentration camp accompanied by SS guards

in fact, anyone who was seen as a political dissident. Storm troopers had begun raiding Berlin's famous gay bars during the Weimar Republic. Later, male homosexuals were sent to concentration camps, where the SS made them wear yellow armbands, then pink triangles. Some 20,000 Jehovah's Witnesses were imprisoned when they failed to swear allegiance to the state or refused to register for the draft or omitted to say 'Heil Hitler', while all Roma people (gypsies) were persecuted on racial grounds.

T-4 Euthanasia Programme

In October 1939, Hitler authorized the T-4 Euthanasia Programme. He slyly backdated the order to 1 September, so that it would appear to be a wartime measure.

'War is the best time for the elimination of the incurably ill,' said Hitler. They were a burden on the *Volk*, he thought, and an embarrassment to those claiming to be a 'master race'.

In fact, the murder of the physically and mentally disabled, the incurably ill and the elderly had started long before. Soon after Hitler came to power, the Minister of Health in Bavaria proposed sending anyone he considered 'inferior' to the concentration camps, including the mentally retarded. Then medical institutions began withholding medical treatment and food from selected individuals.

The T-4 Programme – so called because the chancellery offices that ran it were based at Tiergartenstrasse 4 in Berlin – became systematized under Dr Karl Brandt, one of Hitler's personal physicians, and Philipp Bouhler, the head of the chancellery. They were charged with expanding the 'authority of physicians… so that patients considered incurable, according to the best available human judgment of their state of health, can be granted mercy killing'.

Dr Leonardo Conti and Dr Karl Brandt, keen supporters of the Nazis' euthanasia programme – the eradication of so-called 'useless eaters'

The two leaders of the programme began by ordering a survey of psychiatric institutions, hospitals and homes for the chronically ill, thereby effectively co-opting the entire medical establishment.

The programme's administrators did not bother to examine anyone, or read their medical records. Instead, they decided whose lives were 'unworthy of living' by reading the forms that had been sent to them by institutions throughout Germany.

Those who believed in eugenics, a fashionable view at the time even in Britain and the United States, became enthusiastic about the programme. Nazism was seen as Darwinism in action. However, many people were put to death just because they were seen to be economically unproductive. The Nazis referred to them as 'useless eaters'.

Karl Brandt was an enthusiastic proponent of the Nazis' euthanasia programme from the very start. After completing his training as a doctor in 1928, he joined the Nazi Party in

1932 and the SA in the following year. Under the 1933 Law for the Prevention of Hereditarily Diseased Offspring he began performing abortions on numerous women who were considered to be genetically disordered, mentally or physically handicapped or racially deficient. It was thought that their children could inherit their conditions.

His career took a leap forward when he treated Hitler's adjutant, SA Lieutenant-General Wilhelm Brüchner, after a car accident. His grateful patient introduced him to Hitler's inner circle. In 1939, he was appointed co-director of the T-4 Euthanasia Programme and three years later he became Reich Commissioner for Sanitation and Health, and an SS major-general.

As the war drew to a close, Hitler was furious when he discovered that Brandt had sent his wife and children towards the American lines so they would not be captured by the Soviets. Brandt was arrested, tried and sentenced to death. Only the intervention of

A 'planning meeting' for recaptured territories in the East, attended by (from the left) Hess, Himmler, Bouhler, Dr Todt, Heydrich and others

Himmler and Speer stopped the sentence being carried out. Captured by the Allies, Brandt was again sentenced to death when an American court found him guilty of having approved medical experiments in the concentration camps. His defence was that 'any personal code of ethics must give way to the character of total war'. Unfortunately for him, the court did not see things his way. His speech from the scaffold was cut short by the black hood that was placed over his head.

Philipp Bouhler was a skilled administrator who could organize Hitler's correspondence or the killing of people with the same consummate ease. Wounded in the First World War, Bouhler joined the Nazi Party in 1921. His first job was with the *Völkischer Beobachter*, the Party newspaper. Then in 1933 he became a member of the Reichstag, before succeeding Himmler as police chief in Munich. After making a success of his time in Munich he was called to Berlin, where he became head of Hitler's chancellery and chairman of the censorship committee. During that time he published *Fight for Germany* and *Napoleon: A Genius's Cometary Path*, one of Hitler's favourite books.

Finally, in 1939, he became co-director of the T-4 Euthanasia Programme. He and his wife

committed suicide after being captured by the Americans at the end of the war. The game was up and they knew it.

At first, the victims of the T-4 Programme were killed by starvation and lethal injection but later they were gassed. Chambers disguised as showers were built at six killing centres in Germany and Austria – Bernburg, Brandenburg, Grafeneck, Hadamar, Hartheim and Sonnenstein. SS personnel in charge of the transport of the prisoners donned white coats in order to maintain the illusion that it was a medical procedure. Relatives were informed when the 'patients' were transferred, but they were not allowed to visit them. They were later furnished with a death certificate, a letter of condolence and an urn containing the ashes.

Doctors and psychiatrists were able to save a few of their patients – but only if they co-operated by sending replacements. While the Church had remained silent on the 'Jewish question', the bishop of Münster, Count Clemens August von Galen, vehemently protested about the 'mercy killings', arguing that all life was sacred. Opposition grew so strong that Hitler was jeered by an angry crowd for the only time in his 12-year reign. This incident resulted in the official cancellation of

Stutthof concentration camp in Poland (near Danzig) took in Polish Jews from Warsaw and Bialystok as well as from the Baltic states

the T-4 Programme on 24 August 1941. By then, at least 70,000 people had been killed. But the programme continued as part of the escalating Holocaust. In all, some 200,000 people lost their lives because of the T-4 Programme.

Targeting the Jews

While the Nazis had done their utmost to rid Germany of its Jews, the rapid expansion of the Third Reich had brought another two million Jews under the control of the SS. There were so many of them that the *Einsatzgruppen* could not cope, so on 21 September 1939 Heydrich ordered the establishment of the *Judenräte* – councils made up of leading Jewish citizens and rabbis. The *Judenräte* were made personally responsible for carrying out German orders. There was little choice because failure meant death.

Two months later, Jews were forced to identify themselves by wearing the Star of David. Jewish schools were closed, Jewish organizations were dissolved, property was seized and men were conscripted into forced labour.

The Jews were then forced into ghettos. There were around 400 ghettos in Poland alone, the largest of them being the Warsaw Ghetto. Thirty per cent of the city's population was forced into 2.4 per cent of its area. The population density of the ghetto reached over 200,000 per square mile, with an average of 9.2 people to a room. As if this were not enough, the ghetto was sealed off from the rest of the city in the autumn of 1940. Food was supplied but it was not enough to sustain life, so starvation and disease took their inevitable toll before the systematic extermination of the Jews began. Following the invasion of the Soviet Union in June 1941, the *Einsatzgruppen* began the methodical task of murdering all of the Jews in the newly conquered territories. By the end of the year, 80 per cent of the Jews in Lithuania had been killed. The mass murder of around a million Jews, including virtually all Jewish males of arms-bearing age, was also occurring in Belarus, Estonia, Latvia, Ukraine, Moldova and most of the Russian territory west of the line that ran from Leningrad to Rostov.

The first trainloads of German, Austrian and Czech Jews rolled eastwards to killing sites in the Ostland

Hitler made Himmler responsible for 'security' behind the lines and he also gave the SS the authority to implement settlement plans in the occupied Soviet Union. It was a project that was dear to Himmler's heart.

The Final Solution

On 31 July 1941 Göring authorized Heydrich, then chief of the RSHA, to co-ordinate the resources of the Reich 'for a total solution of the Jewish Question in the area of German influence in Europe'. In the following six months, the first trainloads of German, Austrian and Czech Jews rolled eastwards to killing sites in the so-called Reich Commis-sariat, Ostland. The Soviet Jews were already being systematically annihilated.

Department IV B4 of the RSHA, led by Adolf Eichmann, directed local police agencies to round up all Jews inside the Reich. It then organized the required railway trains through the director of German State Railroads and the Reich Ministry of Transport. The shooting of the Jews was handled by regional security police forces and SD commanders.

Adolf Eichmann was yet another casualty of the Great Depression who had found steady employment with the Party, even if it was the chief executioner's job. Born in Solingen, Germany, he moved with his family to Linz in Austria, Hitler's favourite city, during the First World War. In 1932, he joined the Nazi Party and the SS and in the following year he joined the terrorist school of the Austrian Legion in Lechfeld.

Two years later he was attached to the SS unit at Dachau and then he joined the SD's Berlin office as an expert on Jewish affairs.

His first plan was to rid Europe of its Jews

Adolf Eichmann joined the SS in 1932 and went on to play a major role in organizing the deaths of millions of Jews

The *SS-Sturmbrigade Dirlewanger*, whose members were largely ex-convicts and psychopaths, trains its sights on the Warsaw Ghetto

by sending them to Palestine. He even went so far as to attempt to meet the Arab leaders in Palestine, but his efforts were blocked by the British authorities. With Palestine out of the running he went off to Vienna in 1939. Within a short time the whole of the city's Jewish population had been transported to Poland. Large numbers died on the rail journey and when the survivors arrived, they discovered that no food or housing had been provided for them.

Eichmann performed a similar task in Prague in the following year. When the RSHA was established, he was rewarded by being made head of the Jewish affairs section. It was rumoured that he had Jewish relatives and had even kept a Jewish mistress when he had lived in Vienna. Whether this was true or not, such a thing would have fitted in well with the Nazis' double standards.

In 1945, he was captured by United States troops, but he escaped from his prison camp. He managed to get to Argentina, where he settled in 1958, but two years later he was kidnapped by Israeli secret service agents and smuggled out of the country. At his trial in Tel Aviv, he denied responsibility for the mass killings.

'I had orders,' he said, 'but I had nothing to do with that business.'

He was only responsible for the transportation, he maintained.

'I never claimed not to know about the liquidation,' he said. 'I only said that department IV B4 had nothing to do with it.'

He was squeamish about the gassing, he said, after observing a gassing van in operation at Chelmno.

'I didn't look inside. I couldn't. Couldn't! What I saw and heard was enough. The screaming and … I was much too shaken.'

Odilo Globocnik planned the liquidation of the Warsaw Ghetto and, in total, was responsible for the deaths of an estimated 1.5 million people

After that he kept his distance.

'I was horrified. My nerves aren't strong enough. I can't listen to such things … without them affecting me.' Eichmann was sentenced to death all the same.

On 20 January 1942 Heydrich invited 15 key officials from various Reich ministries, including Adolf Eichmann, to a conference at a lakeside villa in the Berlin suburb of Wannsee. At the Wannsee Conference, as it became known, he presented plans 'to implement the desired final solution of the Jewish Question'. He informed the delegates that Hitler had authorized the operation and had designated the SS to co-ordinate a European-wide 'Final Solution policy'. He impressed upon them that the success of such an unprecedented operation depended on the active participation of their agencies.

The word extermination was never used during the conference, but the intention was clear. An earlier plan of deporting the Jews to Madagascar was dismissed as impractical during wartime. Instead, all of the Jews in Europe would be rounded up and sent east,

where they would be used as forced labour. Their working and living conditions would be so hard that a large number of them would die of 'natural diminution'. Those who survived this harsh regime would be 'treated accordingly'.

Heydrich summed up the situation:

Another possible solution of the problem has now taken the place of emigration – that is, the evacuation of the Jews to the east… Such activities are, however, to be considered provisional actions, but practical experience is already being collected which is of the greatest importance in relation to the future final solution of the Jewish problem.

Indeed, practical experience had been gathered by SS men during the gassing of innocent victims in the T-4 Programme. At Chelmno in western Poland, the systematic gassing of prisoners using gassing vans had begun on 8 December 1941, just hours after the Japanese had attacked Pearl Harbor. But while the suffering of the victims was of little concern to the SS guards, there were more practical considerations. The vans only had a limited capacity, the process was slow and unloading them was 'unpleasant'.

Extermination camps

In October 1941, SS and police leader Odilo Globocnik received a verbal order from Himmler to start work on the construction of an extermination camp at Belzec. Others would follow at Sobibor and Treblinka. Permanent gas chambers would be installed in the camps.

When they arrived, victims would be separated by sex before being stripped of their clothing. They would then be herded into the gas chambers, where they would be killed by exhaust gas from diesel engines, which would be pumped through pipes in the ceiling. The bodies would then be removed by parties of camp inmates, the *Sonderkommando*, who would plunder gold teeth, dentures and other valuables from the corpses and then take the bodies to the crematoria or dump them in mass graves. Members of the *Sonderkommando* were murdered and replaced periodically in order to remove any potential witnesses to the scale of the mass murders.

In 1943, there were uprisings at Sobibor and Treblinka and the gassings stopped. The extermination of the Polish Jews, known as Operation Reinhard, was almost complete, so Himmler ordered that the remaining prisoners be shot and the camps closed down. Forty-two thousand Jewish forced labourers at the Trawniki, Poniatowa and Majdanek camps were also shot. Globocnik wrote to Himmler: 'I have completed Operation Reinhard, and have dissolved all the camps.'

Born in Trieste, Globocnik moved to Austria with his family during the First World War. He joined the Nazi Party in 1930 and the SS in 1933. It was around that time that he was thought to have been involved in a jewel robbery, during which a Jewish jeweller was murdered. Soon afterwards, he became deputy *Gauleiter* of Austria.

After the *Anschluss* Hitler appointed him *Gauleiter* of Vienna, but he was dismissed for illegal currency speculation in 1939. After that, he was made to serve as a member of the *Waffen-SS* during the invasion of Poland. However, Himmler did not like to see talent going to waste so he promoted Globocnik to SS and police leader of the Lublin district, with the added responsibility of annihilating the Polish Jews. Globocnik was responsible for the liquidation of the Warsaw Ghetto, which contained around half-a-million Jews, and the Bialystok Ghetto, where another 15,000 Jews were being held. As head of the death camp organization, he was responsible for the deaths of at least another 1.5 million innocent people from other parts of Europe.

Globocnik oversaw forced relocations, exploited slave labour and stole the property of those he murdered in the extermination camps. In September 1943, he transferred to Trieste as SS and police leader for the Adriatic coast, where he persecuted the Italian Jews and the Yugoslav partisans. He was captured by the British in Austria in 1945, when he committed suicide.

While Globocnik and the other SS men were clearing the Polish ghettos and transporting their inmates to the death camps, Eichmann was shipping the Jews out of western Europe. The most notorious camp was Auschwitz. It was, in fact, three camps. Auschwitz I was the original camp, which served as an administrative centre for the whole complex. Established on the orders of Himmler in April 1940, Poles, Jews and Soviet prisoners of war were held there. They had to work in the associated

A Warsaw Ghetto photo used by Jürgen Stroop to illustrate his report for Himmler; the boy is thought to be Tsvi Nussbaum, who survived the Holocaust

arms factory and were ruled over by brutal *Kapos*, usually German criminals. The camp also contained a punishment block, which dispensed various kinds of torture. Sometimes four men would be made to stand all night in a tiny cell or prisoners would be kept without food or water in the basement until they died. There were also sealed cells, where prisoners would gradually suffocate. Other victims would be left hanging with their arms behind their backs for hours, or days, which dislocated their shoulders.

On 3 September 1941, deputy camp commandant SS Captain Fritzsch experimented on 600 Russian prisoners of war and 250 Polish inmates by cramming them into the basement

of Block 11 and gassing them with Zyklon B, a highly lethal cyanide-based pesticide. After that, Zyklon B was used in the gas chambers of Auschwitz II, the extermination camp that was also known as Birkenau.

Having joined the Nazi Party and the SS in 1930, Fritzsch became a guard at Dachau in 1934. In May 1940, he became the first deputy commandant of Auschwitz, which was then just a concentration camp. Fritzsch was sadistic, even by SS standards. Each time an inmate escaped he made sure that ten prisoners were starved to death in the basement of the punishment block. He also enjoyed psychological torture. On one occasion he set up a Christmas tree in the roll-call square. It was hung with lights and there were 'presents' under it – but the presents were the bodies of prisoners who had died while working or who had frozen to death during roll-call.

After being transferred to Flossenbürg in 1942, Fritzsch was arrested and charged with corruption and murder. His sentence was to be sent to the front line with *SS-Panzergrenadier-Ersatzbatallion 18*. Nothing more was heard of him.

Begun in October 1941, Auschwitz II played a major part in the 'Final Solution'. The SS built 300 wooden barracks, four large bath houses where prisoners were gassed, 'corpse cellars' for storing bodies and cremating ovens where the bodies were burnt.

Another camp called Buna-Monowitz, later Auschwitz III, was built nearby in May 1942. This housed slave labour for a chemical and synthetic rubber works which had been built by IG Farben at a cost of 700 million Reichsmarks. Other German corporations built factories with a similar forced labour requirement. Forty-five subcamps were built to house these workers.

It was at Auschwitz that one of the most callous and evil medical practitioners of all time conducted his hideous experiments. While studying philosophy in Munich in the 1920s, Josef Mengele came under the influence of the racial ideology of Alfred Rosenberg. He went on to take a medical degree and then joined the SA in 1933. In the following year he joined the research staff of the newly founded Institute for Hereditary Biology and Racial Hygiene.

From November 1940 to early 1941, Dr Josef Mengele worked for RuSHA in Department II of its Family Office, where he was responsible for the 'care of genetic health' and 'genetic health tests'. When the war started Mengele served as a medical officer with the *Waffen-SS*

Three of a kind: (from the left) Richard Baer, Josef Mengele and Rudolf Höss in relaxed mode at Auschwitz concentration camp

in France and Russia, but in 1943 Himmler appointed him chief doctor at Birkenau, the extermination camp at Auschwitz.

When new batches of prisoners arrived at Auschwitz, Mengele first of all selected a number of likely victims for his cruel experiments. It was then his task to decide who was to live and who was to die. He was known as the 'Angel of Death', or sometimes the 'White Angel', because he wore a white coat and stood on a platform with his arms outstretched, overlooking the new arrivals. After giving them a cursory glance, he directed them to go left to the gas chambers or right to join the forced labour squads, where they at least had a slim prospect of survival. Young children, their mothers and the old and infirm would be sent directly to the gas chambers, while the young and able-bodied would be sent to work. But inadequate food, poor shelter and minimal sanitation soon destroyed the health of those who had been sent into slavery. Once they were unfit for employment, they would be sent back to Birkenau to be gassed.

On one occasion, a mother did not want to

Former SS guards are forced to load the bodies of their victims on to a lorry after the liberation of Bergen-Belsen concentration camp, 1945

be separated from her 13-year-old daughter, so she bit and scratched the face of the SS man who tried to force her to her assigned line. Mengele drew his gun and shot both the woman and the child.

As a blanket punishment he sent everyone to be gassed, including those who had been selected for work, with the comment: 'Away with this shit!'

When it was reported that one block was infested with lice, Mengele sent every one of its 750 female occupants to be executed. He also performed hideous medical experiments on some of the inmates. His favourite subjects were twins. He injected blood taken from one twin into another twin of a different blood type and then recorded the reaction. The recipient of the blood invariably suffered a searingly painful headache and a high fever that lasted for several days. His experiments were as diverse as they were evil. In order to determine if eye colour could be genetically altered, Mengele had dye injected into the eyes of several subjects. This resulted in painful infections and blindness. If his victims died, Mengele would harvest their eyes and pin them to the wall of his office. Young children were placed in isolation cages, and subjected to a variety of stimuli to see how they would react. Several twins were castrated or sterilized. Many twins had limbs and organs removed in macabre surgical procedures performed without an anaesthetic. Other twins were injected with infectious agents to see how long it took to succumb to various diseases. These and other gruesome procedures had no medical purpose, other than to show the supposed superiority of 'Aryans'.

Strangely enough, some child survivors remember him as a kind man, even though he had killed their parents. He gave them sweets and he was their protector, because he wanted to ensure that the prison guards did not maltreat his medical subjects.

In 1945, Mengele surrendered to the Americans, initially using his own name.

If his victims died, Mengele would harvest their eyes and pin them to the wall of his office

Treated as a normal prisoner of war, he was given papers in the name of Fritz Hollmann before being released. He then worked as a farmhand before escaping to Argentina in 1949, taking with him his 'research notes' from Auschwitz. After Adolf Eichmann was captured by Israeli agents in 1960, Mengele fled to Paraguay. He then moved to Brazil where he took the name Wolfgang Gerhard. In 1979, he suffered a stroke while swimming and he drowned. His body was exhumed in 1985 and identified as that of Mengele.

Curiously, there was an unusually high incidence of twins in a village named Cândido Godói in Brazil, which Mengele visited repeatedly. Many of them had blond hair and blue eyes. Brazilian scientists have discounted the theory that Mengele had been continuing his experiments there, but others are not so sure.

Between 1.1 and 1.5 million people died at the hands of the SS at Auschwitz. Ninety per cent of them were Jews. Some 83,000 Poles died there too, along with 19,000 Roma (gypsies).

As the Soviet armies advanced into Poland, the camp was abandoned. In January 1945, 60,000 prisoners were marched to Wodzislaw, where they were put on freight trains – some in open cars – and moved west. Many were shot, or died of hunger or exposure, along the way. When the Red Army arrived, only 7,650 were still alive.

CHAPTER EIGHT
The SS in Retreat

The SS rose to power on the coat-tails of the Nazi Party. But as Germany's star began to fade, the SS had more to lose than any other Nazi organization. Defeat would uncover the murderous crimes of the Holocaust. So the *Waffen-SS* threw itself back into battle. Better to die fighting than die on the gallows.

Wilhelm Bittrich (left) with Hermann Fegelein: Bittrich criticized the Nazi Party but lived to tell the tale; Fegelein was a playboy and womanizer

ALTHOUGH THE GERMAN army had failed to take Moscow in 1941, the *Waffen-SS* had covered itself in glory, both in the Balkans and in the Soviet Union. From March 1942 onwards it was further expanded by the creation of two new divisions.

The first of them was the 7th *SS-Freiwilligen Gebirgs* (Mountain) *Division Prinz Eugen*. Formed from conscripted ethnic Germans in occupied Serbia, Croatia, Hungary and Romania, its purpose was to undertake anti-partisan operations in the Balkans.

After that the *SS-Kavallerie* Brigade was expanded to form the *SS-Kavallerie Division Florian Geyer*. The new division was commanded by SS Major-General Wilhelm Bittrich, but a year later he was supplanted

by SS colonel, later major-general, Hermann Fegelein.

Wilhelm Bittrich managed to be a dedicated SS soldier and a critic of the Nazi Party at the same time. What's more, he lived to tell the tale.

During the First World War, he fought as an officer and trained as a pilot. Eager to take advantage of his training, he joined the SS in 1932 so that he could fly with SS Flying Echelon 'East'. He continued flying under an agreement with the Soviets, which circumvented the aviation ban imposed by the Treaty of Versailles.

Bittrich joined the SS-VT in 1934 and the *Leibstandarte* in 1939, commanding the *Deutschland* regiment in Poland and France. In January 1942, he fell ill and was forced to step down but he had recovered by May, when he took command of the *SS-Kavallerie* Brigade, expanding it into a division. He went on to command the *Das Reich* and *Hohenstaufen* divisions. As commander of *II SS-Panzer Korps* he was responsible for the defeat of the Allies at Arnhem in 1944, the last victory that the *Waffen-SS* would see. He was then decorated, even though he had been implicated in the July Plot to assassinate Hitler and had been marked for death by Himmler because of his unflattering comments about the Nazi regime. His last wartime task was the defence of Vienna. Arrested in 1945, he was tried by the French for war crimes, but he was acquitted in 1954.

Hermann Fegelein, a playboy and a womanizer, was the complete opposite of the steady Bittrich. After serving as a stable boy for Christian Weber, one of the original members of the Nazi Party, he enlisted in the 17th Cavalry Regiment in 1927. He went on to join the SA in 1930 and the SS in 1931.

It might have been Fegelein's boyish good looks that made Himmler favour him, or it could have been his smooth, ingratiating manner. Whatever it was, the *Reichsführer* made sure that Fegelein's career moved onwards and upwards. In 1937, he became head of the SS Main Riding School that Himmler had established in Munich and while serving in the Polish campaign he formed the first *Waffen-SS* cavalry unit from the *SS-Totenkopfverbände*. After being wounded three times in action behind the lines in Russia he was awarded the Knight's Cross. Later, Himmler gave him command of the *SS-Kavallerie Division Florian Geyer*.

In June 1944 he married the sister of Hitler's mistress and short-lived wife, Eva Braun, which enabled him to move yet deeper into Hitler's charmed circle. Then as Himmler's personal adjutant to Hitler, he was wounded in the July Plot, which raised his status even further. But by April 1945 he could see that Germany was going to lose the war. Charmed circle or not, he did not intend to go down with the sinking ship. One day, Hitler suddenly noticed that Fegelein had left the *Führerbunker*. He was found at his home in civilian clothes, carrying a large amount of foreign currency and some of Eva Braun's jewellery. It was obvious that he was preparing to escape with his Hungarian mistress.

When he was taken back to the bunker, Eva Braun begged for his life on the grounds that her sister was pregnant. Nevertheless, a court-martial was ordered. Although the evidence of his desertion was clear, Fegelein was drunk and raving, and was considered unfit to stand trial. However, he suffered a stroke of bad luck when the news came that Himmler was trying to make peace with the Allies. As Himmler's 'golden boy', Fegelein was held responsible for his patron's treachery. According to some reports, he was then shot.

The struggle in the east

Hitler met with more resistance than he had bargained for when he invaded the Soviet Union on 22 June 1941. The Red Army was ill-equipped and unprepared but it had two allies. One was the Russian autumn rains and the other was a civilian population that would fight to the bitter end. By the end of 1941 the Soviet Union was bloodied but unbowed. The bitter fighting between the two nations would last until 1945.

Stalingrad might have been lost, but the SS still managed to make its presence felt in other areas. In one famous incident, the Red Army attempted to bottle up the German 16th Army at Demyansk, south of Leningrad. The intention was to cut the Germans off from the Staray Russa railway, so that they had no lines of supply. Beginning in January 1942, the Red Army devoted every available man and machine to the encirclement of the *SS-Totenkopf Division*, five *Wehrmacht* infantry divisions and numerous German auxiliary divisions. But SS men were trained to fight to the death if need be. After months of bloody fighting the *SS-Totenkopf* Division finally managed to hack its way through the opposing armour. The *Totenkopf*'s commander, SS Lieutenant-General Theodor Eicke, was awarded the Oak Leaves to the Knight's Cross. The *SS-Totenkopf Division* was then withdrawn to France, where it underwent reorganization and retraining along with *Das Reich* and the *Leibstandarte*.

When they had been honed into battle-readiness, the three divisions were formed into *I SS Panzer Korps*, which was rushed to the Eastern Front in January 1943, just as the *Wehrmacht* was being crushed at Stalingrad. SS Lieutenant-Colonel Joachim Peiper formed a battalion from the *Leibstandarte* and rescued the *Wehrmacht*'s 320th Infantry Division at Kharkov, earning the Knight's Cross.

The son of an army officer, Peiper volunteered for duty with the *Leibstandarte* in 1934 and then attended *Junkerschule* at Brunswick. He was Himmler's adjutant from 1938 to 1939. When war broke out, he served in the *Leibstandarte*, a motorized regiment, during the campaign in western Europe.

The Soviets bitterly denounced Peiper's 'blowtorch battalion'. The force had acquired its name by attacking enemy-held villages at night, when its troops fired indiscriminately and set the straw roofs alight. Peiper was accused of similar tactics in Italy. When he returned to the Eastern Front as commander of the 1st SS Panzer Regiment, he won the Oak Leaves to his Knight's Cross, but he was again accused of burning villages and killing

Former adjutant to Himmler, Joachim Peiper: wherever he went, soldiers under his command were accused of terrible war crimes

Paul Hausser (in glasses to Himmler's left) near Kharkov in 1943 – *Das Reich*'s commander was known as 'the father ("Papa") of the *Waffen-SS*'

prisoners. His savagery was even-handed though. In Belgium, he executed five young German recruits for looting, making the others march past the corpses.

The 1st SS Panzer Regiment also saw action in Normandy, when Peiper suffered a nervous breakdown. However, he was back in action for the Battle of the Bulge, when men of his unit murdered over 100 American prisoners of war. After the war, Peiper and 73 others were tried for the massacre. Forty-three of them, including Peiper, were condemned to death. Fortunately for him, his sentence was commuted to life imprisonment and he was released in 1956. But fate eventually caught up with him. Twenty years later, he was murdered when his home was set on fire. It is thought that the perpetrator was a former member of the French Resistance.

Battle of Kharkov

Following the surrender of the German Sixth Army at Stalingrad, the SS Panzer Corps was in full retreat. Hitler ordered it to 'stand fast and fight to the death' at Kharkov, but SS Lieutenant-General Paul Hausser was convinced that his tanks would be annihilated if they were trapped in the city. Disobeying Hitler's order, he pulled his unit out and turned it round to face the enemy. Another order came

to encircle Kharkov from the north, but only a direct attack was going to save the day. Without any support from the *Luftwaffe*, the Panzer Corps smashed through the Soviet line.

After four days of savage house-to-house fighting, Kharkov was recaptured by the *Leibstandarte* in March 1943. The offensive cost the Red Army an estimated 70,000 casualties, while the SS Panzer Corps lost around 44 per cent of its strength. Hausser was eventually pardoned for his disobedience and was awarded the Oak Leaves to his Knight's Cross.

Paul Hausser never wanted to be anything other than a soldier. He was a military cadet at the age of 12. Commissioned in 1899, he served as a staff officer during the First World War. He stayed on in the *Reichswehr* at the end of the conflict, rising to become a colonel. After retiring in 1932 he joined Stahlhelm, a right-wing veterans' organization, which was incorporated into the SA and then the SS. Hausser transferred to the SS-VT in 1934, becoming an inspector of *SS-Junkerschule* in 1935 and a brigadier in 1936.

Known as 'Papa' to his men, Hausser fought in Poland and France, commanding the Second SS Division *Das Reich*. During the advance into Russia he lost an eye – a black eye patch became his trademark – and won the Knight's Cross. In Normandy, in 1944, he was injured again when he led the break-out from the Falaise Gap, winning the Oak Leaves with Swords. Promoted to general and colonel-general (a special rank) of the *Waffen-SS*, he commanded Army Group G, ending the war on Field Marshal Kesselring's staff. At the Nuremberg Trials he vigorously defended the military role of the *Waffen-SS* and denied any involvement in wartime atrocities. When he was released in 1948, he attempted to re-establish the reputation of the SS, claiming that the foreign units of the SS were really the precursors of the NATO army.

The Third Battle of Kharkov, as it was called, ended on 15 March 1943 and two days later Joachim Peiper's 'blowtorch battalion' raced to take control of Belgorod. Now was the time to eliminate the Kursk salient – that is, the point at which the Soviet line jutted westwards for some 80 miles. The plan was to cut off the Soviet forces in the salient by making two pincer attacks at its neck. II SS Panzer Corps, part of 4 Panzer Army, was chosen to spearhead the northward offensive. The attack penetrated to a depth of 22 miles (35km) before it was stopped by the Soviet 1st Tank Army. Despite appalling losses, the Soviet tank armies held the line. This was the prelude to the Battle of Kursk, the largest tank battle in history. Despite all of its efforts, the II SS Panzer Corps was prevented from making its expected

During the advance into Russia, Hausser lost an eye and won the Knight's Cross... in Normandy he was injured again

breakthrough and by 13 July the Soviets had won a decisive victory.

The *Leibstandarte* Division was still in fighting trim after Kharkov, so when the Allies invaded Italy in September 1943, the *Leibstandarte* was pulled out of Russia and sent to Italy to join the *16 SS-Panzergrenadier Division Reichsführer-SS*. When the Italians surrendered, the *Leibstandarte* began disarming Italian units. On 19 September, the German High Command heard reports that elements of the Italian Fourth Army were regrouping in Piedmont, near the French border, so Peiper's 3rd Battalion was sent to demilitarize them. Arriving in the province of Cuneo, Peiper was met by an Italian officer who warned him that his forces would attack unless Peiper's unit left the province immediately. Peiper refused, which goaded the Italians into action. The veterans of Peiper's battalion defeated the Italians in a fierce battle and then disarmed the remaining Italian forces in the area.

Clearing the Warsaw Ghetto

The *Waffen-SS* had to do more than face the enemy. Sometimes the force was directed against German citizens. This was the case when the Warsaw Ghetto was ordered to be cleared in 1942. It is estimated that 320,000 Jews, 30 per cent of Warsaw's population, were crammed into this small district. Between

In his element: Jürgen Stroop (in peaked cap) watches the mayhem grow all around him as the Warsaw Ghetto goes up in flames

23 July and 21 September the Nazis shipped 265,000 Jews to Treblinka, where they were gassed. That meant 55,000 people were left in the ghetto. On 9 January 1943, Himmler visited Warsaw and ordered the deportation of another 8,000 Jews. However, the people that were selected did not report as ordered. Instead, they concealed themselves in prepared hiding places. The Jewish resistance had managed to obtain some pistols, a few rifles and one machine gun from the Polish Home Army (AK), so they had something to retaliate with. Over the next three days, a large number of heavily armed German troops swarmed into the ghetto. If they thought it was going to be a pushover they were wrong. The Jews had nothing to lose so they fought fiercely and without personal regard. In the end, the

now 1,500 strong, who fired at them and threw homemade bombs that even destroyed a couple of tanks. The Germans responded with flame-throwers. The resistance fighters resorted to the sewers, defying all attempts to burn, smoke or flood them out. They kept up their resistance until 16 May, when their ammunition ran out. It had taken 28 days to remove the remaining 40,000 Jews, with some 7,000 shot. Others died in the flames or committed suicide. The Germans reported 16 dead and 85 wounded. After supervising the dynamiting of the Great Synagogue of Warsaw, an exultant SS Major-General Jürgen Stroop wrote a report entitled: 'The Warsaw Ghetto is no more.'

If anyone saw himself as a member of the 'master race' it was Stroop. After volunteering to fight in the First World War, he won the Iron Cross Second Class and was wounded. He joined the Nazi Party and the SS in 1932 and was made an auxiliary policeman. Promoted rapidly, he served in the Sudetenland.

After the invasion of Poland, Stroop was transferred to Poznan as the head of *Selbstschutz*, the notorious 'self-defence' formation of the local ethnic Germans. In 1941, he served on the Eastern Front with the infantry regiment of the 3rd *SS-Totenkopf* Division, where he was awarded a clasp to the Iron Cross and an Infantry Assault Badge in bronze.

In September 1942, he was promoted to SS brigadier and was made inspector of the SiPo and SD in south Russia.

Stroop's hatred of Jews was well known, so on 17 April 1943 he was sent to Warsaw as a replacement for SS and police leader *SS-Oberführer* Ferdinand von Sammern-Frankenegg, who had been court-martialled for 'defending Jews'. Sammern-Frankenegg was sent to Croatia, where he was killed by Yugoslav partisans. Stroop systematically

soldiers managed to remove around 5,000 Jews – but at a cost of 20 dead and 50 wounded.

It was Hitler's birthday on 20 April and Himmler had come up with the perfect present. A special ghetto clearance operation was just what his *Führer* wanted. On 19 April, 821 *Waffen-SS* Panzergrenadiers from five reserve and training battalions and one cavalry reserve battalion moved in, along with some *Wehrmacht* units. They were met by a resistance that was

Himmler's greatest departure from the Aryan ideal came when he persuaded Hitler to form a Bosnian Muslim division

cleared the Warsaw Ghetto against stiff resistance and then sent his lavishly illustrated report to Himmler, who proudly showed it to Hitler. In Himmler's eyes, Stroop's attack on the Jews had been the equal of any military campaign and it deserved to be honoured as such. Accordingly, Stroop was awarded the Iron Cross First Class at a gala reception in Warsaw.

He was then posted to Greece where he directed the deportation of Jews to Auschwitz. Captured in Bavaria in the uniform of an infantry officer, he was found to be carrying false papers. After a short trial he was convicted of the summary execution of Allied airmen in the area of his command and was sentenced to death. He was sent to Poland to be executed. Unrepentant to the last, he sat in his cell and joyfully recalled the destruction of Warsaw's Great Synagogue.

'What a wonderful sight! I yelled out, "Heil Hitler!" and pressed the button. A terrific explosion brought flames right up to the clouds. The colours were unbelievable. An unforgettable allegory of the triumph over Jewry.'

Convicted of war crimes, he was executed publicly on the site of the former ghetto.

Expanding the *Waffen-SS*

By 1943, Himmler was beginning to realize that the tide was turning against Germany. What the Fatherland needed was more SS troops in the field – and quickly. Whole divisions, not battalions, were added at full speed. This was nothing new, however. Over the course of the war the *Waffen-SS* grew from three elite divisions of German-born Aryans to an international force that comprised 41 divisions and many other units. *Waffen-SS* numbers never exceeded 10 per cent of the total strength of the German army, but its troops were far more deadly than those of its larger rival.

Foreign nationals had begun to join the ranks of the *Waffen-SS* in 1941, when the *SS-Nordland* Regiment had been formed from Danish and Norwegian volunteers. Building on that earlier success, Himmler pulled *SS-Panzergrenadier-Regiment Nordland* out of the line in February and used it as the basis for the 11th *SS Volunteer Panzergrenadier Division Nordland*. Divisions were also formed in France and later in the year volunteers from the Hitler Youth were brought into the 12th SS Panzer Division *Hitlerjugend*.

Scandinavian and French nationals were one thing, but Himmler's greatest departure from his Aryan ideal came when he managed to persuade Hitler to let him form a Bosnian Muslim division. The 13th *Waffen* Mountain Division of the *SS-Handschar* (1st Croatian) was created to fight Tito's Yugoslav partisans.

After that, a division was formed from volunteers in Galicia – the part of Poland that

Volunteers of the Muslim *SS-Handschar Division* receive Nazi indoctrination in the form of a booklet entitled *Islam and Judaism*, 1943

was absorbed into Ukraine after the Soviet invasion of 1939. But Himmler could not afford to sit around waiting for volunteers. There was a war to fight. Compulsory military service was introduced to the Reich Commissariat of Ostland and the 15th *Waffen* Grenadier Division of the SS (1st Latvian) was raised. By the time the 16th *SS-Panzergrenadier Division Reichsführer-SS* had been created back in Germany the *Waffen-SS* had expanded from eight divisions to sixteen.

They were sorely needed. By this time the Allies were getting closer. When they landed at Anzio in January 1944 the 16th *SS-Panzergrenadier Division Reichsführer-SS* sent a battle group to meet them. It was followed by the *Brigata d'Assalto, Milizia Armata*, which was known to the Germans as the 1st *Italienische Freiwilligen Sturmbrigade*. The brigade performed so well that a delighted Himmler declared that it was to be fully integrated into the *Waffen-SS*.

Despite a few local successes the war was going badly for Germany, so the *Waffen-SS* was expanded again in 1944. Conscripts and volunteers were pulled from the Germans'

occupied territories and a number of *Waffen-SS* divisions were hastily created. Ostland was again plundered for conscripts. First of all, Latvia had to yield up its remaining men of fighting age and then Estonia was forced to supply enough troops for a division. In the Balkans, the 21st *Waffen* Mountain Division of the SS Skanderbeg (1st Albanian) was created from Albanian and Kosovan volunteers.

The speed at which some of these non-German divisions were raised was matched by the length of their basic training. Raw troops were often sent into battle after receiving only two or three weeks' instruction and many units were issued with miscellaneous items of captured equipment. On top of all of that, officers and men shared a mixture of languages in some forces, which sometimes made vital communications difficult. Even so, some divisions managed to perform exceptionally well, even by SS standards.

Then a second *Waffen-SS* cavalry division, the 22nd SS Volunteer Cavalry Division *Maria Theresia*, was formed. The bulk of its men were ethnic German conscripts from the Hungarian army. Another Netherlands division was then created, followed by a polyglot division that was really the size of a brigade. The 24th *Waffen Gebirgs Division der SS* was made up of ethnic German volunteers from Italy, with other volunteers from Slovenia, Croatia, Serbia and Ukraine. Its primary purpose was to fight partisans on the frontiers of Slovenia, Italy and Austria, where the mountainous terrain required specialist troops and equipment.

Himmler then ordered the Hungarian defence minister to form the 25th *Waffen* Grenadier Division of the SS *Hunyadi* (1st Hungarian) and the 26th *Waffen* Grenadier Division of the SS (2nd Hungarian). The divisions consisted mainly of Hungarian and Romanian volunteers, though one regiment from the Hungarian army was ordered to join them. Another division that saw action on the Hungarian Front was the 31st SS Volunteer Grenadier Division, which was formed from conscripted ethnic Germans, mainly from the Batschka region of Hungary.

In Belgium sufficient volunteers were found to create two further divisions, one from the Flemish-speaking north and the other from the French-speaking south. To add to the cosmopolitan nature of the *Waffen-SS* the 30th *Waffen* Grenadier Division of the SS (2nd Russian) was formed in East Prussia from Ukrainian, Belarusian, Russian and Polish

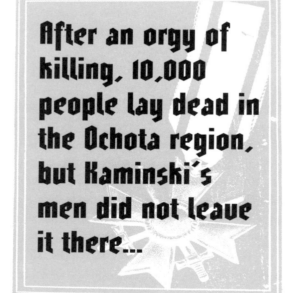

After an orgy of killing, 10,000 people lay dead in the Ochota region, but Kaminski's men did not leave it there...

collaborators, while fresh Italian volunteers who wanted to fight for the Germans were formed into the 29th *Waffen* Grenadier Division of the SS (1st Italian).

Plans to convert the Kaminski Brigade into the 29th *Waffen* Grenadier Division of the SS RONA (1st Russian) were dropped after the execution of its commander, Bronislav Kaminski.

Kaminski served in the Red Army during the Russian Civil War (1918–20) and then returned to civilian life. Although he appears to have been leading an ordinary existence in 1937, he became a victim of Stalin's Great Purge. After being arrested as a 'counter-revolutionary' he was exiled to Bryansk Oblast, a Russian province. He harboured an understand-able grudge against his homeland at that point, so he joined the anti-partisan militia when the Germans invaded, becoming its head in 1942. As a reward for co-operating with the Germans, he was allowed to establish the autonomous administra-tion of Lokot. His orders were to conscript all able-bodied men, including Russian 'volunteers' from a nearby concentration camp. Kaminski's troops were armed with discarded Soviet equipment, while uniforms were supplied by the Germans.

By January 1943, Kaminski had assembled nearly 1,000 men, together with eight tanks and three armoured cars. His force was called the Russian National Liberation Army (RONA).

It took part in the attack on the Kursk salient in July 1943 and it also committed a number of atrocities against civilians. Needless to say, several attempts were made on Kaminski's life.

In February 1944 Kaminski's men were evacuated to Belarus. At that point his second in command tried to defect to the partisans, after being offered an amnesty for his entire regiment. Kaminski displayed his absolute devotion to the Reich by strangling his subordinate in front of his men, followed by eight other mutineers. An admiring Himmler awarded him the Iron Cross. After Kaminski's unit had been renamed the *Volksheer-Brigade Kaminski* in his honour, his troops undertook more anti-partisan operations. The brigade then became part of the *Waffen-SS*. It was renamed as the *Waffen-Sturm-Brigade RONA*, and Kaminski was given the rank of *Waffen-Brigadeführer der SS*, the only man to hold such rank. Himmler was so impressed by the performance of the unit that he decided to turn the brigade into the 29th *Waffen-Grenadier-Division der SS (russische Nr.1)*. Kaminski was promoted again, this time to *Waffen* brigadier and *Waffen-SS* major-general.

The Warsaw Uprising of August 1944 changed everything for Kaminski. Still called the *Waffen-Sturm-Brigade RONA*, his brigade was sent off to assist in the suppression of the Warsaw rebels. After an orgy of savage killing, 10,000 people lay dead in the Ochota area alone, but Kaminski's men did not leave it there. Himmler received reports that they had indulged in extensive looting and had raped two German women. The *Reichsführer-SS* used this as an excuse to court-martial Kaminski and have him shot. Looted property belonged to the Reich – that is, to Himmler. Kaminski's men were told that their commander had been killed by Polish partisans, but they did not believe the story.

Fighting on two fronts

By 1944 Germany was fighting against Great Britain and the United States in the west and the Soviet Union in the east. Hitler had always been aware that fighting on two fronts was nothing but suicidal. In fact, the Molotov–Ribbentrop Pact had been designed to avoid that very possibility, back in 1939.

The Eastern Front was a huge theatre of war in its own right. Although the Allies were now involved, Germany's main fight was with the Soviet Union. SS units were sent in all directions, often covering huge distances to get to the point of battle.

In January 1944, six German divisions, including the 5th SS *Wiking*, the 5th SS Volunteer *Sturmbrigade Wallonien* and the Estonian SS Battalion *Narwa*, were encircled by the Red Army in a defensive position along the Dnieper River in Ukraine. Just as the German troops were getting ready to go down fighting, the *1 SS-Leibstandarte* thundered to the rescue, after travelling some distance. The *Leibstandarte* kept the Soviets occupied while the trapped divisions made their escape.

The 500th SS Parachute Battalion and the 7th SS *Prinz Eugen* were deployed far to the south as part of Operation *Rösselsprung* (Knight's Move in chess). Their objective was the capture of partisan leader Josip Broz Tito, who was thought to be hiding in the cave headquarters of the Yugoslav partisans near Dravr. The troops launched an offensive in April and May 1944, but by the time they fought their way into the cave Tito had fled.

Right up in the north III SS (Germanic) Panzer Corps in Army Group North fought along the Narva – a river in Estonia – in July and August 1944, during the retreat from Leningrad. SS Lieutenant-General Felix Steiner commanded volunteer SS units from Norway,

Denmark, the Netherlands and Belgium, along with conscript SS units from Latvia and Estonia. Stalin had planned to retake Estonia and use it as a base for attacks on Finland and East Prussia, but the stiff resistance of the German troops delayed the Soviet effort in the Baltic by seven-and-a-half months.

In the meantime, the D-Day landings were one of Hitler's major preoccupations. The Allies' plans were unknown so I SS Panzer Corps *Leibstandarte SS Adolf Hitler* was moved to Septeuil, 25 miles (40km) west of Paris.

From that position it could move quickly to the coast when the invasion began. The corps comprised the 1st *SS-Leibstandarte SS Adolf Hitler*, the 12th *SS-Hitlerjugend*, the 17th *SS-Götz von Berlichingen* and the *Wehrmacht*'s Panzer-Lehr-Division.

Normandy Landings

On the day of the Normandy landings, 6 June 1944, many German leaders were taken by

Members of the *SS-Panzer-Division Hitlerjugend*: (from the left) Kurt Meyer, Franz Witt and Maz Wünsche, near Caen in June 1944

surprise. The first *Waffen-SS* unit in action was the 12th *SS-Hitlerjugend*, which arrived in the Caen area on 7 June. SS Brigadier Kurt Meyer made Ardenne Abbey his headquarters. Twenty-seven captured Canadian soldiers of the North Nova Scotia Highlanders and the 27th Canadian Armoured Regiment were taken there and shot. Their bodies were not discovered until the Canadian Regina Rifle Regiment liberated the abbey in the following month.

The massacre would come back to haunt Meyer at the end of the war. After serving with the Mecklenburg police, Meyer joined the *Leibstandarte* in Berlin in 1934. He saw service in the campaigns in Poland and France before going to Greece, where he led his reconnaissance battalion from the front – this earned him the nickname '*Schnelle* (Speedy) Meyer'. Otherwise he was known as 'Panzermeyer', because he was said to be as tough as a battle tank.

While commanding a reconnaissance detachment in the Balkans and Russia, Meyer earned the Knight's Cross and the German Cross. In 1943 he was given command of the 12th SS-Panzer Division *Hitlerjugend*, which he led in an aggressive bid to halt the Allied invasion in June 1944. He was wounded on 6 September and captured at Amiens on 17 November, where he fell into the hands of Belgian partisans. Perhaps fortunately for him, he was rescued by the Americans and handed over to the British.

After the war, he was brought before a Canadian military court where he was charged with the massacre of the Canadian prisoners. Although he was convicted and sentenced to death by firing squad, the sentence was commuted to life imprisonment. After being transferred to West Germany, he was released in 1954.

Other German units arrived in Normandy in

The Oradour-sur-Glane massacre

ON 10 June, the 2nd *SS-Division Das Reich* arrived at the town of St Junien, 12 miles (19km) from Oradour, where it encountered the local Maquis. The troops marched on to Oradour, where they surrounded the village and ordered everyone to assemble in the market square.

At about three o'clock, the women and children were locked in the local church while the men were formed into groups before being taken to local garages and barns, where they were shot. Finally, the church was blown up and then set on fire. Those who attempted to escape were shot.

In 1953 a French military court established that 190 men, 245 women and 207 children had been murdered. The SS troops at Oradour were commanded by SS Major Otto Dickman, but he had been killed in action in the Normandy battle area, so the court looked further down the line. Twenty members of his company were convicted and sentenced to death, though only two were executed.

the days that followed the landings.

On 11 June, the 17th *SS-Götz von Berlichingen* arrived, coming into contact with the United States 101st Airborne Division. Then the 1st *SS-Leibstandarte* arrived at the end of the month. The division defended the village of Carpiquet and its aerodrome against the Canadian troops who were trying to break out of the beachhead.

The only other *Waffen-SS* unit in France at this time was the 2nd *SS-Das Reich*, which was based at Montauban, north of Toulouse. It was ordered to move north. On its way it passed through Tulle in central France, where the Maquis had killed 139 members of the German garrison. As was often the case, the local population would pay the price. The SS rounded up all men between the ages of 16 and 60. Ninety-nine of them were tortured and hanged and the rest were sent as slave labour to Dachau concentration camp, where most of them died. On the next day *Das Reich* reached Oradour-sur-Glane, where it massacred 642 French civilians.

Over the days that followed the Allied landings further SS units such as II SS Panzer Corps were rushed to Normandy. The force had arrived from the Eastern Front on 26 June, just in time to counter another Allied attempt to break out of the eastern end of the beachhead, but in the absence of further reinforcements the *Waffen-SS* was hard pressed to stop the Allied

advance. Its efforts were studded with costly failures such as Operation *Lüttich*, which sought to prevent the American forces from leaving the western end of the beachhead. The 1st *SS-Leibstandarte* and the 2nd *SS-Das Reich* took part in the campaign, losing half of their tanks.

In one bloody incident the Americans managed to trap the 1st *SS-Leibstandarte*, the 10th *SS-Frundsberg*, the 12th *SS-Hitlerjugend* and the 17th *SS-Götz von Berlichingen* in the Falaise pocket, while the 2nd *SS-Das Reich* and the 9th *SS-Hohenstaufen* were on the outside. At this stage there was a gap through which the German forces could make their escape. The *Das Reich* and the *Hohenstaufen* were ordered to attack Hill 262 in order to keep the Falaise gap open, but despite all of their efforts the gap had been closed by 22 August. All of the German forces inside the pocket were dead or in captivity. The fighting around Hill 262 alone cost 2,000 dead and 5,000 prisoners. The 12th *SS-Hitlerjugend* had started the campaign with almost 20,000 men and 150 tanks but by the end of the battle it was down to 300 men and 10 tanks.

With the German army in full retreat, two more *Waffen-SS* formations were sent to the battle in France – *SS-Panzergrenadier Brigade 49* and *SS-Panzergrenadier Brigade 51*, which had been formed from staff and students at the

SS-Junkerschulen. At the beginning of August they held the crossings over the Seine southeast of Paris, which allowed the army to retreat. The few survivors were incorporated into the 17th *SS-Götz von Berlichingen.*

SS barbarity

While the crucial battles were being fought in France or on the Eastern Front, the 4th *SS-Polizei Panzergrenadier Division* was stationed in Greece. On 10 June its troops went on a bloody two-hour rampage in the village of Distomo. Running from door to door they massacred a large number of Greek civilians, supposedly in revenge for a partisan attack. In all, 218 men, women and children were killed. According to survivors, the SS forces 'bayoneted babies in their cribs, stabbed pregnant women and beheaded the village priest'. An internal enquiry was told that the troops had not been fired on, but it still exonerated their commander, SS Captain Fritz Lautenbach. After the war, no one was prosecuted, but West Germany paid Greece 115 million Deutschmarks in restitution.

The troops of the 16th *SS-Panzergrenadier Division Reichsführer-SS* were no less barbarous when they were conducting anti-partisan operations in Italy. On 12 August 1944, a battalion entered the village of Sant'Anna di Stazzema. All of the able-bodied men fled into the woods while women, children and the elderly were herded into barns and stables, where they were murdered with machine-guns and hand grenades. The victims included some 110 children. The youngest, Anna Pardini, was only three weeks old. Eight pregnant women were killed. One of them, Evelina Berretti, had her baby pulled from her womb before she was shot. All of the livestock were also killed and the village was burned. The SS men then

> ## SS forces 'bayoneted babies in their cribs, stabbed pregnant women and beheaded the village priest'

unconcernedly ate their lunch nearby. After the war the divisional commander, SS Major-General Max Simon, was the only person to be held to account. However, in 2005, ten former members of the SS were found guilty in absentia and sentenced to life imprisonment. The name of the officer in charge, SS Captain Anton Galler, was only discovered in 1999. He had died six years earlier. There was more carnage to come from the 16th *SS Reichsführer-SS.* Between 29 September and 5 October 1944 its men systemically murdered more than 800 people in the vicinity of Marzabotto in the Apennines. The officer in charge, SS Major Walter Reder, reported the 'execution of 728 bandits'. But many of these 'bandits' were children – 45 were less than 2 years old and 110 were under 10. The SS troops had also killed 142 men over 60 years old, 316 women and five Catholic priests. Reder was prosecuted immediately after the war and in 2007 another ten former SS men were convicted in absentia.

Max Simon was also accused of being

involved in the Marzabotto killings, but how much control he had over the troops in his division is not known.

After winning the Iron Cross in the First World War, Simon joined the *Freikorps* and then the *Reichswehr*. A protégé of Theodor Eicke, he joined the Nazi Party and the SS in 1933. After serving as commandant of the Sachsenburg concentration camp, he raised the 1st *SS-Totenkopfstandarte Oberbayern*, becoming its colonel. The regiment was involved in the *Anschluss* and the occupation of Czechoslovakia and Simon also fought in the Battle of France and the invasion of Russia.

He was given command of the newly formed 16th *SS-Panzergrenadier Division Reichsführer-SS* in October 1943. In July 1944, the division moved into Italy to fight the British in the Arno sector and undertake anti-partisan operations. Simon was awarded the Oak Leaves to the Knight's Cross and the German Cross in Gold at that time. He was then given command of the XII SS Corps, which surrendered to the Americans in Bavaria in May 1945.

After a trial, Simon was sentenced to death by a British court for the murders that had been committed by his troops, including those in Marzabotto, but his punishment was commuted and he was released in 1954. Several further attempts were made to prosecute him in Germany, without success.

However, the officer in charge of the 16th *SS Reichsführer-SS* at the time of the Marzabotto massacre, Major Walter Reder, was certainly guilty of murder. Born in the Sudetenland, Reder was already a member of the Hitler Youth when he joined the SS-VT in 1934. He was then sent to the *SS-Junkerschule* at Brunswick before being put in command of various *Totenkopf* units.

Reder participated in the invasion of Poland

Max Simon was accused of being involved in the Marzabotto killings, but his death sentence was commuted and he was released in 1954

and won an Iron Cross. During Operation
Barbarossa, he commanded a regiment that
spearheaded the advance on Leningrad.
Injured during the Third Battle of Kharkov,
he lost the lower part of his left arm. When he
recovered, he commanded a battalion at the
liquidation of the Warsaw Ghetto. He was then
posted to northern Italy, where he oversaw the
Marzabotto massacre.

Subsequently captured by the Americans,
Reder was released because of his war wounds,
but he was then re-arrested and transferred to
the British lines.

Finally, he was sent to Italy, where he was
sentenced to life imprisonment. Following
a number of petitions for clemency he was
released in 1985, after writing a letter of
apology to the citizens of Marzabotto. He was
greeted by the Minister of Defence, a member
of the far-right Austrian Freedom Party, when
he returned to Austria, after which he quickly
rescinded his apology.

As 1944 progressed, the German forces
were becoming even more stretched, with
units scurrying here and there to face constant
new challenges.

In Finland, the 6th *SS-Gebirgs Division
Nord* held the line during the Soviet summer
offensive and then it formed the rearguard for
the three German corps in an epic 1,000-mile
(1,600km) march to Mo i Rana in Norway.

In early September 1944, the II SS Panzer
Corps was pulled out of the line in Belgium
for a refit, so it was in the Arnhem area of
the Netherlands just as the Allies launched
Operation Market Garden. The Training and
Reserve Battalion of the 16th *SS Division
Reichsführer-SS* was also in the area. Together
they ensured that the Allied airborne operation
was a failure. The city of Arnhem was not
liberated until 14 April 1945.

Warsaw Uprising

Meanwhile, the *Waffen-SS* was dealing with
the Warsaw Uprising. Between August and
October 1944, the *Waffen-Sturm-Brigade RONA*
and the *Dirlewanger Brigade* were sent to
Warsaw to put down the mutiny. Hitler had
ordered the city to be razed, so the SS troops
could be as barbarous as they chose. During
the battle, the *RONA* was responsible for the
Ochota massacre, but the *Dirlewanger* behaved
even more atrociously. Encouraged by their
commander *SS-Oberführer* Oskar Dirlewanger,
who told them to take no prisoners, the
Dirlewanger troops looted, gang-raped women
and children, played 'bayonet catch' with
live babies and tortured captives by hacking
off their arms, dousing them with petrol and
setting them alight to run flaming down the
street. The soldiers' behaviour was so bad that
even Himmler became alarmed. He ordered a
battalion of SS military policemen to stand by,
in case the *Dirlewanger* troops turned on their
own leaders or on nearby German units.

The original members of the *Dirlewanger
Brigade* were convict poachers (they recruited
from jails), so the unit was at first called the
Wilddiebkommando Oranienburg (Poacher's
Command Oranienburg). At first it carried out
anti-partisan duties in Poland. A short time
later, Himmler made Oskar Dirlewanger the
group's commander. It then became part of the
Waffen-SS, at which point it began to recruit
criminals whose crimes were so serious that
they were not allowed to serve in penal battalions. Sensing potential freedom, many inmates
from the concentration camps volunteered
and patients from mental hospitals were also
admitted. By September 1940 the formation
numbered about 9,000 men and its name was
changed to *SS-Sonderbatallion 'Dirlewanger'*.

The force was involved in so many cases of

Oskar Dirlewanger was a convicted paedophile who found a home in the SS. The men under his command were the lowest of the low

rape, theft, looting and indiscriminate killing in Poland that the General Government's SS and police leader, Friedrich Krüger, had it transferred to Belarus, where it is estimated that along with the Kaminski Brigade it burned 200 villages and murdered 120,000 people, mostly civilians.

Like many others, Oskar Dirlewanger found a home in the SS when things were going badly for him in the outside world. Much decorated and wounded during the First World War, Dirlewanger joined the *Freikorps* and then fought in the Ruhr and Upper Silesia. In 1922, he graduated with a degree in political science, joining the Nazi Party in the following year. But he had personal failings. After serving

two years in prison for paedophilia, he was convicted again of the same offence and sent to a concentration camp. Fortunately for him, his friend Gottlob Berger obtained his release. After a period in the Spanish Foreign Legion, Dirlewanger joined the German Condor Legion, which had been formed to fight for General Franco in the Spanish Civil War.

In 1939, Dirlewanger was finally redeemed when Berger secured him a commission in the SS. Dirlewanger then persuaded Berger to let him set up a special unit that would be recruited from convicted criminals. As befitted a former convict and sexual deviant, Dirlewanger encouraged his men to behave in the most brutal fashion. He did not do badly himself. First of all he gave his troops permission to loot and then he shot them so that he could take their plunder for himself. During the Warsaw Uprising, it is said that he entertained the mess with the death throes of young Jewish girls, whom he had injected with strychnine.

After the uprising had been put down, Dirlewanger's brigade was transferred to Slovakia where there was a national revolt in progress. In the last weeks of 1944, the *Dirlewanger Brigade* was sent to the front in northern Hungary, but so many men deserted to the Russians that the unit had to be withdrawn. However, it was soon reinforced, becoming the 36th *Waffen* Grenadier Division of the SS. The new unit met with no more success than its predecessor, being forced to surrender when it was encircled southeast of Berlin.

By then an *SS-Oberführer*, Dirlewanger was wounded and sent to the rear, where he was captured by the French. His next stop was the Altshausen jail, where he was beaten and tortured. It is unclear whether he died at the hands of the Polish guards or former members of his own brigade.

The Ochota massacre

AT 10 am on 4 August 1944 the *Waffen-Sturm Brigade* RONA moved into the Ochota district of Warsaw. Its first target was Opacze-wska Street, where it expelled the inhabitants, shooting the elderly or anyone that was reluctant to leave. The flats were then looted and set on fire. As the mayhem spread, the troops of the *RONA* murdered people in allotments and threw grenades into basements where people were hiding. By the following day, thousands of people had been expelled from their homes and herded into a makeshift camp. On the way, the men were beaten and the women were raped and murdered.

There was no water, food or medical aid in the camp. Nevertheless, SS Lieutenant-General Erich von dem Bach-Zelewski had the effrontery to issue a favourable report: 'There was nothing wrong there; everything was in order.' Hundreds died and their fellow inmates were forced to carry the corpses to a nearby gymnasium, where they were burned. Others were buried in a pit. A sadistic German officer shot three captured boy scouts as they lowered a body into the mass grave.

The brigade went on to the Radium Institute, which had been founded by Marie Curie for the treatment of cancer. They looted the hospital, gang-raped and murdered the patients and staff and then set fire to the building. Moving on, the troops threw grenades into a Polish field hospital. Over 10,000 innocent civilians died in the *RONA*'s orgy of killing and destruction.

The end of the dream

In late August 1944, the 5th SS *Wiking* was ordered back to Modlin on the Vistula. Fighting alongside the *Luftwaffe*'s *Fallschirm-Panzer Division 1 Hermann Göring*, the unit annihilated the Soviet 3rd Tank Corps. Grouped with the 3rd SS *Totenkopf* in the IV SS Panzer Corps, the SS *Wiking* helped force the Red Army back across the Vistula, where the Eastern Front stabilized until January 1945.

Meanwhile, Hitler was planning a counter-offensive action through the Ardennes in Belgium. On 26 October 1944, the Sixth SS Panzer Army was formed under Sepp Dietrich. It incorporated I and II Panzer Corps, along with Otto Skorzeny's SS Panzer Brigade 150. The aim was to split the British–American line in half and then capture Antwerp. The Panzer Army would then go on to encircle and destroy four Allied armies, thereby forcing the Western Allies to negotiate a peace treaty and join the war against the Soviets.

But supplies were short and the Panzer commanders were told that they would have to capture petrol on the way. Due to stout resistance this proved impossible, so with fuel running short the Germans returned to the retreat on 8 January 1945.

Otto Skorzeny was something of a swashbuckling character. Born in Vienna to a military family, he acquired a prominent duelling scar as a student. After his studies he joined the Austrian Nazi Party in 1931, followed by the SA, so his role in the *Anschluss* was almost inevitable. Skorzeny was working as a civil engineer during Hitler's invasion of Poland in 1939, but the event fired him to volunteer for the *Leibstandarte SS Adolf Hitler.* He went on to fight in the Netherlands, France and the Balkans.

Injured fighting with *Das Reich* on the Eastern Front, he was given permission to form *Oranien-burg*, a special forces unit, at which point he came into his own. In 1943 he parachuted into Iran to stir up dissident hill tribes and then he was personally selected by Hitler to lead the raid to rescue Mussolini. The Italian leader was being held in the Campo Imperatore Hotel on the Gran' Sasso d'Italia, which was only accessible by cable car from the valley below. Skorzeny's men overwhelmed the guard and snatched Mussolini without a shot being fired.

Skorzeny was then involved in two failed operations – Operation Long Jump and Operation *Rösselsprung*. Afterwards, he helped stop a possible mutiny in Berlin after the July 1944 attempt on Hitler's life. Then he kidnapped the son of the Hungarian premier Miklós Horthy, in order to forestall possible peace negotiations with the Soviets.

During the Battle of the Bulge he led a brigade of English-speaking Germans dressed in American uniforms, who created confusion behind the Allied lines. Hitler awarded him the Oak Leaves to the Knight's Cross. He was then put in charge of the Werewolves, a Nazi organization that was formed to engage in guerrilla warfare against the occupying Allies. But Skorzeny soon realized that he had too few men for an effective fighting force so he set up the 'ratlines' – secret routes for smuggling Nazis out of Germany.

On 16 May 1945, he surrendered to the Americans and was tried for his improper use of American uniforms during the Ardennes Offensive. However, he was acquitted when the court was told that the British Special Operations Executive had done a similar thing by dressing in German uniforms. While awaiting 'denazification' he escaped and went to live in Spain, where he continued his clandestine activities.

By late December 1944 the German forces began running out of steam. The Allies were just too numerous and too widespread. The Siege of Budapest was just one indication of the turning tide. IX *Waffen* Mountain Corps of the SS (Croatian) and other Axis forces were encircled in Budapest. In an attempt to rescue them, the IV SS Panzer Corps – the 3rd *SS-Totenkopf* and the 5th *SS-Wiking* – attacked the Soviet 4th Guards Army, but the superior Soviet forces halted them

The swashbuckling Otto Skorzeny next to Benito Mussolini (in black) after freeing the former Italian dictator from captivity in 1943

just 17 miles (27km) from Budapest. The city surrendered on 13 February 1945.

Although the war was almost over, the *Waffen-SS* continued to expand. In January the 32nd SS Volunteer Grenadier Division was formed from the remnants of other units and staff from the *SS-Junkerschules* and in February the *Waffen* Grenadier Brigade of the SS Charlemagne (1st French) was upgraded to a division, as was the SS Volunteer Grenadier-Brigade *Landstorm Nederland*. SS police units transferred to the *Waffen-SS* became the 35th SS and Police Grenadier Division, while the *Dirlewanger Brigade* was reformed as the 36th *Waffen* Grenadier Division.

But there were few new volunteers or conscripts for the *Waffen-SS*, so units from the *Wehrmacht* were attached to bring it up to strength. Another ploy was to bring together the remnants of failed divisions. The 37th SS Volunteer Cavalry Division *Lützow* was formed

Peiper's troops? Remarkable film captured from a German soldier included this image of desperate-looking SS men heading for Malmédy

in this way. In the end, the only reasonable sources of recruits were again the *SS-Junker-schules*. The 38th SS Division *Nibelungen* was formed by conscripting the remaining students and staff. Even so, the force contained only around 6,000 men, the strength of a normal brigade.

On 15 January 1945, the XIII SS Army Corps joined the last major counter-attack in the west through Alsace and Lorraine. Ten days later, they were on the retreat again.

Things were going no better on the Eastern Front. In February 1945, the Eleventh SS Panzer Army assembled in Pomerania and then attacked the advancing 1st Belorusian Front, but it was repulsed by the Red Army. III (Germanic) SS Panzer Corps was pulled back to Stargard and then Stettin, which is located on the Oder. From there, joined by the X SS Corps, it launched another offensive. In early March, the force was encircled by the Soviets, who hit them relentlessly with everything at their disposal. By 8 March the last 8,000 men had surrendered.

After the failure of the Ardennes Offensive, Hitler decided to launch a final major offensive

on the east, so the 6th SS Panzer Army was refitted. Its numbers were boosted by drafting in raw recruits and men from the now defunct *Luftwaffe* and *Kriegsmarine*. Support would be provided by the IV SS Panzer Corps. For the first time ever, six SS Panzer divisions were taking part in the same offensive. The attack, known as Operation Spring Awakening, took place in the Lake Balaton area in Hungary. It took the Soviets completely by surprise. Fortunately for them, they had been massing 1,000 tanks for an assault along the Danube valley, so they had a large, fully prepared tank force to hand.

It was the Germans' turn to be shocked. The German advance quickly ground to a halt. There was little that the 6th SS Panzer Army could do with less than 50 per cent of its strength and no prospect of reinforcements.

Hitler was furious. The 1st *SS-Leibstandarte* had not fought 'as the situation demanded', he screamed. He then ordered the troops to remove their 'Adolf Hitler' cuff bands, but Sepp Dietrich did not relay the order to his men.

The 6th SS Panzer Army withdrew towards Vienna where the II SS Panzer Corps, under

Massacre at Malmédy

LEADING the German advance guard in the Ardennes was General Joachim Peiper. At Honsfeld in Belgium his men shot 19 GIs and robbed their dead bodies before moving on to an airfield near Bullingen where they forced a group of captured Americans to refuel their tanks. Afterwards, Peiper shot them in cold blood. Eight more prisoners of war were killed at Ligneuville and 100 American prisoners were machine-gunned in Malmédy. By some miracle 20 Americans managed to escape. They hid in a café but Peiper's men soon found them.

Without further ado the building was set on fire and they were machine-gunned when they ran out. A triumphant Hitler imagined that the news of these massacres would demoralize the American troops, but the opposite was the case. It gave them an incentive to fight back.

Wilhelm Bittrich, faced the Red Army. Vienna fell on 13 April after Bittrich's II SS Panzer Corps had pulled out to avoid encirclement.

All hope for the Germans had gone as the Red Army closed in on Berlin, but Hitler still believed that the city could be saved and the Nazi dream could yet become reality. However, Hitler's health was deteriorating quickly and he did not realize that he was directing divisions that had long gone. Nevertheless, he managed to muster III (Germanic) SS Panzer Corps, and on 16 April the remnants of the 11th SS-Nordland, the 33rd SS-Charlemagne and the Spanish Volunteer Company of SS 101 were sent as support.

A week later, Hitler appointed SS Brigadier Wilhelm Mohnke as commander of the central sector of Berlin, which included the Reich chancellery. Mohnke's command post was underneath Hitler's bunker. He had been given the job because he had been injured in an air raid, which meant that the Leibstandarte had to leave him behind when it went to Hungary. His first task was to form Battle Group Mohnke from the Leibstandarte Flak Company, the Leibstandarte Training and Reserve Battalion, the Führer-Begleit Company and the 600-strong Reichsführer-SS Begleit Bataillion. Its core group, though, was the 800-strong Leibstandarte Guard Battalion, which was normally assigned to guard Hitler.

As befits a soldier who defended Berlin to the end, Mohnke was a fervent Nazi. One of Hitler's original Stabswache, he became a founder member of the Leibstandarte in 1933. He was wounded during the Polish campaign, when he was awarded the Iron Cross.

However, Mohnke had a barbarous side to his character, which emerged when he started to take command. For example, he was the leader of the 2nd Battalion of the Infanterie-Regiment SS-Leibstandarte when its troops massacred 80 British prisoners of war at Wormhoudt during the Battle of France. He was wounded again in the Balkans, losing part of his foot on the first day of the campaign, but he rejoined the Leibstandarte in Russia. In 1943, he was transferred to the newly formed 12th SS Panzer Division Hitlerjugend.

Mohnke was responsible for further atrocities in France. When his regiment was in Normandy, he interrogated three captured Canadians. Afterwards, they were taken into a bomb crater and shot, while Mohnke looked on. He was implicated in four similar incidents, which resulted in the murder of nine other Canadians. By December 1944 Mohnke was commander of the Leibstandarte. He was the one who issued the order to take no prisoners at Malmédy.

Mohnke was in Hitler's bunker when he committed suicide on 30 April 1945 and he was seen to weep openly. On the following day he set fire to the bunker and joined an escape group. Captured by the Soviets, he was one of the first German prisoners of war to be released in October 1955. It seems that he got away with his crimes.

Only two weeks before Hitler's suicide, there were plans to escort him in a breakout. On 16 April 1945 the remnants of the 11th *SS-Freiwilligen-Panzergrenadier Division Nordland*, commanded by SS Brigadier Joachim Ziegler, were ordered back into Berlin for that purpose.

Ziegler had served with the Condor Legion in Spain before fighting in Poland, the Low Countries and France, winning the Iron Cross. In June 1943, he was transferred from the *Wehrmacht* to III (Germanic) SS Panzer Corps and was granted permission to wear an SS uniform. Just over a year later, in July 1944, he was given command of the 11th *SS-Freiwilligen-Panzergrenadier Division Nordland*. In September 1944 Ziegler was awarded the Knight's Cross because of the conduct of his division. Then things started to go wrong. In February 1945, his division joined the offensive in Pomerania, but it was forced to withdraw. It then fought a rearguard action into Berlin where Hitler dismissed him and placed him under arrest in the bunker – though strangely enough he presented him with the Oak Leaves to his Knight's Cross two days later.

After Hitler's suicide, Ziegler was freed. He was trying to negotiate a truce when he was killed near Friedrichstrasse railway station.

Ziegler's replacement as commander of the *Nordland*, Gustav Krukenberg, was a career soldier like Ziegler. Krukenberg met with no more success than Ziegler. On 27 April the *Nordland* was pushed back into the central government district, where it fell under Mohnke's overall command.

After serving as an officer in the First World War, Krukenberg became private secretary to the foreign minister. In 1932 he joined the Nazi Party, where he worked in the propaganda ministry after Hitler came to power. At that time he was a member of the *Allgemeine-SS*. After the outbreak of war, he rejoined the army and then he transferred to the *Waffen-SS* in 1943.

A fluent French-speaker, Krukenberg commanded the *SS-Charlemagne Division*. He was leading the remnants of the unit in the defence of Berlin when he took over the command of the *Nordland* from Joachim Ziegler. When Hitler killed himself, he gathered up the rest of his command and tried to break out. Still friendly with Ziegler, he was with him when he was killed. Krukenberg finally surrendered to the Soviets after hiding out in an apartment for a week.

Nothing could stop the Red Army now, but the troops of the SS had been conditioned to fight until the end. As the Soviets raced to take the Reichstag and the Reich chancellery, they met with stiff resistance. In bloody street fighting the survivors of the 33rd *SS-Charlemagne* held out against overwhelming odds. But there could be no fight without the *Führer*. After receiving news of Hitler's suicide, Mohnke ordered a breakout. What was left of the 11th *SS-Nordland* headed northwest towards Mecklenburg, but the unit faced fierce fighting around the Weidendammer Bridge. A few very small groups managed to reach the Americans on the Elbe, but most could not make it through the Soviet rings. The lucky ones were killed in action – the Soviets were merciless captors.

On 2 May hostilities were officially ended by order of Helmuth Weidling, the *Wehrmacht*'s commandant of Defence Area Berlin. When news of the surrender reached them, some of the remaining SS men shot themselves rather than surrender to the Soviets. They included Mohnke's adjutant, SS First Lieutenant Gert Stehr of the *Führer* Escort Detachment, formerly the *Leibstandarte*.

At the victory parade in Red Square on 24 June 1945, captured standards were displayed. The most prized exhibit was the standard of the *Leibstandarte SS Adolf Hitler*.

Victory celebrations, Red Square, 1945: the Red Army parades captured German banners, including that of the *SS-Leibstandarte Adolf Hitler*

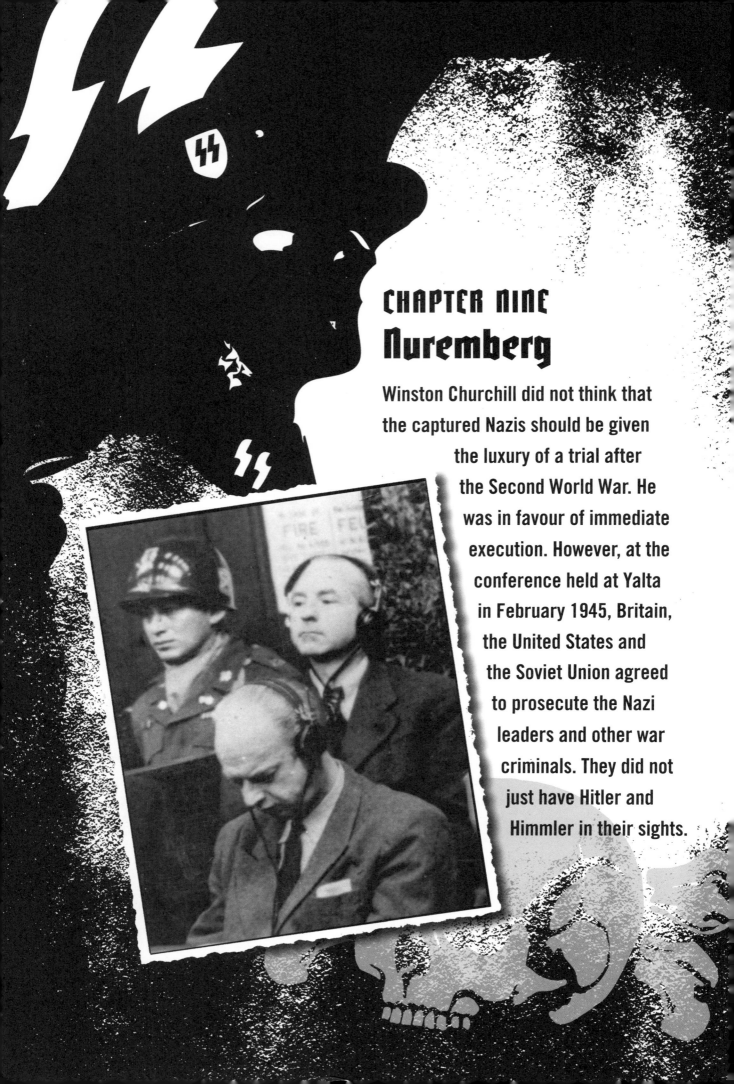

CHAPTER NINE
Nuremberg

Winston Churchill did not think that the captured Nazis should be given the luxury of a trial after the Second World War. He was in favour of immediate execution. However, at the conference held at Yalta in February 1945, Britain, the United States and the Soviet Union agreed to prosecute the Nazi leaders and other war criminals. They did not just have Hitler and Himmler in their sights.

The Palace of Justice in Nuremberg where the trials of Nazis were held, beginning with the major war criminals

AN INTERNATIONAL MILITARY Tribunal was set up by the London Conference in August 1945. It was given the authority to indict offenders on four counts: crimes against peace – planning and initiating wars of aggression; crimes against humanity – genocide, extermination and deportation; war crimes – violations of the laws of war; and conspiracy to commit any of the first three offences. Britain, the United States, the Soviet Union and France would each provide one judge and one prosecutor.

The International Military Tribunal first sat on 18 October 1945, in the Supreme Court Building in Berlin. The prosecution entered indictments against 24 Nazi leaders and six 'criminal organizations' – Hitler's cabinet, the leadership corps of the Nazi party, the SS and the SD, the SA, the Gestapo and the General Staff and High Command of the *Wehrmacht*.

However, Heinrich Himmler, the architect of the SS and the man who has been described as 'the greatest mass murderer of all time', could not be charged. On 23 May 1945 he managed to evade justice, at least in this life, by committing suicide.

The main trial

On 20 November 1945, the tribunal moved to the Palace of Justice in Nuremberg. The building contained some 80 courtrooms and around 530 offices, with the added bonus of a large undamaged prison block. The proceedings were conducted under the presidency of Lord Justice Geoffrey Lawrence (later 3rd Baron Trevethin and 1st Baron Oaksey) and the legal procedures followed Anglo–American common law practice. During the 218 days of the trials, testimony from 360 witnesses was introduced, with 236 witnesses appearing in the court itself.

The Accused – front row (from left): von Weiszäcker, von Moyland, Keppler, Bohle; back row – Dietrich, Berger, Schellenberg, von Krosigk

The histories of those called up for trial were many and various. For example:

FRITZ SAUKEL

Originally a merchant seaman, Fritz Saukel was interned in France during the First World War. He joined the Nazi Party in 1923 and became *Gauleiter* of Thüringia in 1927, later becoming the region's Reich Regent. In 1933 he became a Reichstag member and a year later he was made an honorary lieutenant-general in the SA and the SS. As general plenipotentiary for labour deployment, Saukel imported five million workers into Germany. They were treated harshly, to say the least, but when he was questioned at Nuremberg he denied that they had been used as slave labour or that any deliberate attempt had been made to work them to death. Found guilty of war crimes and crimes against humanity, he went to the gallows protesting his innocence.

RUDOLF HESS

During the First World War, Hess served in the same infantry regiment as Hitler, before transferring to the Imperial Air Corps. After the war he joined the *Freikorps*. He then studied at Munich University under political theoretician Karl Haushofer. While he was there he joined the Thule Society, a *völkisch* and occultist organization that later sponsored the DAP. All of this made him a prime candidate for the fledgling Nazi Party, which he joined in 1920. Jailed after commanding an SA battalion during the Beer Hall Putsch, he served as Hitler's secretary in Landsberg Prison, when he transcribed and edited *Mein Kampf*. When Hitler seized dictatorial powers, he named Hess as his deputy.

With such a background, Hess's subsequent fall from grace seems more than bizarre. On 10 May 1941, he made a solo flight to Scotland and then landed by parachute close to the estate of

Known as 'Shadowman' because he was never far from Hitler, Martin Bormann implemented a slave labour programme for Slavs and Jews

the Duke of Hamilton, whom he had met at the 1936 Olympic Games in Berlin. It is thought that Hess was on an unofficial peace mission. Hitler was incandescent with rage. Hess was suffering from 'pacifist delusions', he snarled. He ordered that Hess was to be shot on sight if he returned to Germany. Hess's captors came to believe that he was insane, but a psychiatrist who examined him testified at Nuremberg that he was of sound mind.

In court he was seen talking to himself, counting on his fingers and laughing for no apparent reason. He claimed that he did not recognize Göring, who asked to be seated away from him. Göring's request was denied. At first, Hess claimed that he suffered from amnesia and remembered nothing of his Nazi past, but during the trial he declared that his memory had returned, removing the possibility of a plea of diminished responsibility. Hess

was convicted of crimes against peace – that is, planning a war of aggression – and conspiracy with other Nazi leaders. He was acquitted of war crimes and crimes against humanity.

KONSTANTIN VON NEURATH

Honorary SS Lieutenant-General Konstantin von Neurath, *Reichsprotektor* of Bohemia and Moravia, was sentenced to 15 years' imprisonment, but he was released in 1954 because of illness. He died two years later.

MARTIN BORMANN

Martin Bormann was called up in the First World War, but by then the conflict was nearly over, so he never saw action. Afterwards he joined the *Freikorps*. In 1924, he was sentenced to a year in prison as an accomplice to the murder of Walter Kadow. His friend Rudolf Höss was jailed for 10 years. Released in 1925, Bormann joined the Nazi Party and became a leading fundraiser. He is thought to have bought police inspector Heinrich Müller's silence when Hitler's niece Geli Raubal was shot, perhaps by Hitler. Envious of the Blood Order decoration – at first only conferred on veterans of the 1923 Beer Hall Putsch – he expanded the qualifications to include himself.

From 1933 to 1941 he was private secretary to Hitler's deputy, Rudolf Hess. He then fulfilled the dual roles of head of the chancellery and private secretary to Hitler, which enabled him to control access to the *Führer*. He witnessed Hitler's marriage and his last will and testament, and he urged the execution of Göring. A worldwide search for his body took place after the war, but the mystery was solved when his remains were unearthed in Berlin in 1973. However, conspiracy theories abounded until 1998, when modern science finally laid all speculation to rest.

Hermann Göring (front row left) finds himself sitting next to Rudolf Hess, who feigned amnesia, in the defendants' dock at Nuremberg

On 1 October 1946, 22 of the original Nuremberg defendants were found guilty and sentenced to death by hanging. They included SS Lieutenant-General Hans Frank, the governor-general of Poland; SS Lieutenant-General Ernst Kaltenbrunner, head of the SD; SS Lieutenant-General Joachim von Ribbentrop, Hitler's foreign minister; racial theorist Alfred Rosenberg; SS Lieutenant-General Fritz Saukel, organizer of forced labour; Julius Streicher, *Gauleiter* in Franconia; and SS Lieutenant-General Arthur Seyss-lnquart, commissioner for the occupied Netherlands.

They were all hanged on the morning of 16 October 1946, in the old gymnasium of the Nuremberg prison. The bodies were cremated and the ashes were scattered in an estuary of the Isar River. SS Lieutenant-General Martin Bormann, a former Nazi party organizer and private secretary to Hitler, was sentenced to death in absentia.

United States tribunals

Although it was originally intended that the International Military Tribunal would sit again, the Cold War had started and there was no further co-operation between the participants. However, more military tribunals took place in the French, British, American and Soviet zones of occupation.

The United States held a series of trials of lesser war criminals, which were called the US Nuremberg Military Tribunals (NMT). As it happened, the Palace of Justice in Nuremberg was within the American zone of occupation, so the United States tribunals took place in the same building as the main trials.

On 9 December 1946, proceedings began against 23 German doctors, who were accused of participating in the Nazi Euthanasia Programme. The trial lasted 140 days. Eighty-five witnesses appeared and 1,500 documents were introduced in evidence. Sixteen doctors were found guilty. Seven of them were sentenced to death and were executed on 2 June 1948. The names of those who were hanged were Viktor Brack, Karl Brandt, Rudolf Brandt, Karl Gebhardt, Waldemar Hoven, Joachim Mrugowsky and Wolfram Sievers.

- After Viktor Brack had worked on the T-4 Euthanasia Programme, Himmler ordered him to find a way of sterilizing Jews so they could be used as slave labour without any fear of them procreating. He tested the procedures on Auschwitz inmates.

- Karl Brandt had been the head of the T-4 Programme, while Rudolf Brandt had handled Himmler's correspondence, including that relating to the Holocaust.

- Karl Gebhardt had been Himmler's personal physician. At Ravensbrück and Auschwitz he had performed brutal surgical procedures on female inmates, opening their skulls or abdomens without an anaesthetic to see how long they could survive. He had also served as the president of the German Red Cross.

- Waldemar Hoven had worked on the T-4 Programme and he had also been a physician at Buchenwald, where he had carried out medical experiments related to typhus and the inmates' tolerance of a serum containing phenol. Many deaths had resulted from this programme.

- Joachim Mrugowsky had been the head of the SS Hygiene Institute in Berlin. He had distributed Zyklon B, a poison that was used in the gas chambers at the death camps and he had overseen Hoven's work at Buchenwald. In addition, he had experimented with poisoned bullets.

- Wolfram Sievers had been the director of the SS Institute for Military Scientific Research, where he had conducted extensive experiments using human subjects. He had also assisted in an anthropological study that had involved the murder of 112 Jews.

Himmler's personal physician, Karl Gebhardt had performed brutal surgical procedures on concentration camp inmates

- SS Major Fritz Fischer had worked in the camp hospital at Ravensbrück, where he had conducted experiments on inmates, infecting them with typhus, smallpox, cholera and other diseases to test the effectiveness of vaccines. He was sentenced to life imprisonment, but he was released in 1954.

- *SS-Oberführer* Helmut Poppendick had been involved in medical experiments on concentration camp prisoners, including those at Ravensbrück. He was sentenced to ten years' imprisonment, but he was released in 1951.

When the doctors had been tried, it was the turn of those who had been involved with the concentration camps.

- In 1947 the United States prosecuted SS Lieutenant-General Oswald Pohl and 17 other SS officers who had directed the WVHA, the organization that had administered the concentration camps. The main charge against them was that they had supervised the arrangements for the 'Final Solution'. Pohl and three of his fellow defendants were sentenced to death by hanging. Three others were acquitted and the remainder were sentenced to be imprisoned for periods that ranged between ten years and life.

- SS Brigadier Otto Steinbrinck was sentenced to six years' imprisonment when he stood trial alongside Himmler's close friend, wealthy industrialist Friedrich Flick. The charge was using slave labour and profiting from property taken from Jews. Flick spent seven years in jail while Steinbrinck died in Landsberg Prison in 1949.

- The production chief at Auschwitz, SS Lieutenant-Colonel Heinrich Bütefisch, was sentenced to six years' imprisonment when he stood trial alongside SS 'supporting member' Christian Schneider, a fellow director of IG Farben, the manufacturer of Zyklon B. Another director, SS Captain Erich von der Heyde, was acquitted.

Fourteen members of the RuSHA (SS Race and Settlement Main Office) were prosecuted for crimes against humanity, war crimes and membership of the SS. They included:

- Ulrich Greifelt, Reich Commissioner for the Strengthening of Germandom (RKFDV) – found guilty on all counts and sentenced to life imprisonment. Died in prison in 1949.
- Rudolf Creutz, deputy to Greifelt – sentenced to 15 years' imprisonment and released in 1955.
- Werner Lorenz, head of the VoMi – convicted of being an SS member, he was sentenced to 20 years' imprisonment and released in 1955.
- Heinz Brückner, VoMi office head – convicted of being an SS member, he was sentenced to 15 years' imprisonment and released in 1951.
- Otto Hofmann, head of the RuSHA – sentenced to 25 years' imprisonment and released in 1954.
- Richard Hildebrandt, successor to Hofmann – sentenced to 25 years' imprisonment and released in 1952.
- Fritz Schwalm, chief of staff of the RuSHA 'Immigration Office' in Lodz – sentenced to 10 years' imprisonment and released in 1951.
- The heads of the Lebensborn, the health depart-

ment and the legal department were convicted only of being members of the SS and were released.

Twenty-four officers of the Einsatzgruppen stood trial. Fourteen were sentenced to death by hanging. The following defendants were hanged on 7 June 1951:

- Erich Naumann, commander of Einsatzgruppe B.
- Otto Ohlendorf, commander of Einsatzgruppe D.
- Paul Blobel, commanding officer of Sonderkommando 4a of Einsatzgruppe C.
- Werner Braune, commanding officer of Sonderkommando 11b of Einsatzgruppe D.

The following defendants had their sentences commuted and were released:

- Walter Blume, commanding officer of Sonderkommando 7a of Einsatzgruppe B.
- Martin Sandberger, commanding officer of Sonderkommando 1a of Einsatzgruppe A.
- Willy Seibert, deputy chief of Einsatzgruppen D.
- Eugen Steimle, commanding officer of Sonderkommando 7a of Einsatzgruppe B and of Sonderkommando 4a of Einsatzgruppe C.
- Ernst Biberstein, commanding officer of Einsatzkommando 6 of Einsatzgruppe C.
- Walter Haensch, commanding officer of Sonderkommando 4b of Einsatzgruppe C.
- Adolf Ott, commanding officer of Sonderkommando 7b of Einsatzgruppe B.
- Walter Klingelhöfer, officer of Sonderkommando 7b of Einsatzgruppe B.
- Heinz Schubert, officer in Einsatzgruppe D.

The following defendants escaped justice because of illness or death:

- Eduard Strauch, commanding officer of Einsatzkommando 2 of Einsatzgruppe A, was handed over to the Belgian authorities and died in hospital in 1955.

- Otto Rasch, commanding officer of *Einsatzgruppe C*, was removed from the trial on medical grounds and died in November 1948.
- Emil Haussmann, officer of *Einsatzkommando 12* of *Einsatzgruppe D*, committed suicide before the arraignment.

The following defendants were sentenced to imprisonment:

- Mathias Graf, an officer in *Einsatzkommando 6* of *Einsatzgruppe D*, was released on consideration of time already served.
- Heinz Jost, commanding officer of *Einsatzgruppe A*, was sentenced to life imprisonment, but was released after ten years.
- Erwin Schulz, commanding officer of *Einsatzkommando 5* of *Einsatzgruppe C*, was sentenced to 20 years' imprisonment but was released after six years.
- Franz Six, commanding officer of *Vorkommando Moscow* of *Einsatzgruppe B*, was sentenced to 20 years' imprisonment but was released after four years.
- Gustave Nosske, commanding officer of *Einsatzkommando 12* of *Einsatzgruppe D*, was sentenced to life imprisonment but was released after ten years.
- Lothar Fendler, deputy chief of *Sonderkommando 4b* of *Einsatzgruppe C*, was sentenced to ten years' imprisonment but was released after eight years.
- Waldemar von Radetzky, deputy chief of *Sonderkommando 4a* of *Einsatzgruppe C*, was sentenced to 20 years' imprisonment but was released.
- Felix Rühl, officer of *Sonderkommando 10b* of *Einsatzgruppe D*, was sentenced to ten years' imprisonment but was released.

The judgement said that the facts of the case

are so beyond the experience of normal man and the range of man-made phenomena that only the most

complete judicial inquiry, and the most exhaustive trial, could verify and confirm them.

The defendants had committed:

a crime of such unprecedented brutality and of such inconceivable savagery that the mind rebels against its own thought image and the imagination staggers in the contemplation of a human degradation beyond the power of language to adequately portray.

The prosecution had put the number of people who had been murdered by these men at one million, but

it is only when this grotesque total is broken down into units capable of mental assimilation that one can understand the monstrousness of the things we are in this trial contemplating. One must visualize not one million people but only ten persons – men, women, and children, perhaps all of one family – falling before the executioner's guns. If one million is divided by ten, this scene must happen one hundred thousand times…

In a separate trial of government ministers, SS Lieutenant-General Gottlob Berger, SS Brigadier Walter Schellenberg and SS Lieutenant-General Richard Walther were convicted for their roles in Nazi Germany.

They were sentenced to imprisonment and released in the early 1950s.

Other Allied trials were held for the SS concentration camp guards. In the western zone of occupied Germany 5,025 people were convicted. Eight hundred and six defendants were given death sentences and 486 of them were carried out. In the Soviet zone of occupation, it is estimated that there were 45,000 trials. Outside Germany, as many as 60,000 people have been convicted of Nazi crimes: 1,214 war criminals were executed in Poland alone.

CHAPTER TEN
ODESSA

There is some doubt that a formal organization called ODESSA – *Organization der Ehemaligen SS-Angehörigen* (Organization of former SS members) – ever existed. However, a number of former SS criminals, including Adolf Eichmann and Josef Mengele, certainly managed to escape from Germany at the end of the war and find their way to South America.

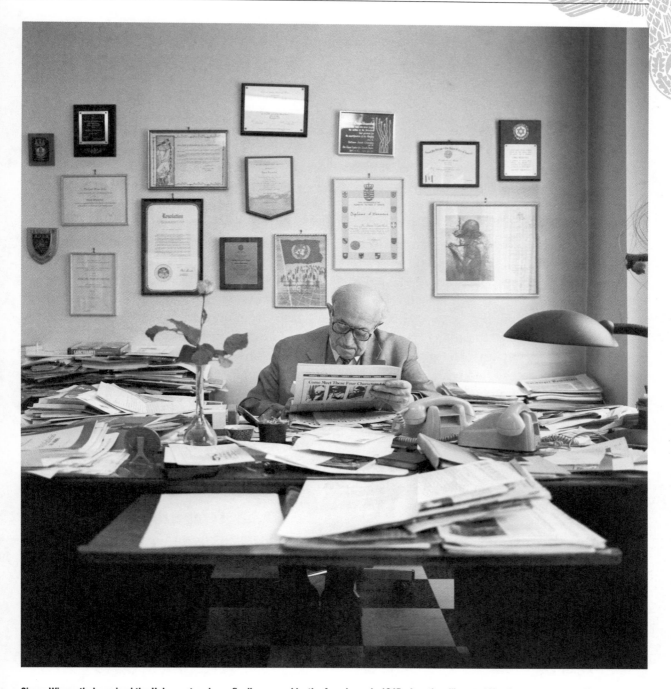

Simon Wiesenthal survived the Holocaust and was finally rescued by the Americans in 1945 when they liberated Mauthausen concentration camp

AZI-HUNTER Simon Wiesenthal learned of the existence of ODESSA while he was talking to former German counter-espionage operatives at the Nuremberg Trials. The United States Army Counter Intelligence Corps (CIC) knew about ODESSA too, and they knew who ran it. According to a top-secret report dated 20 January 1947: 'The leader of this group is Otto Skorzeny, who runs it from the camp at Dachau, where he is interned. The men who take their orders from Skorzeny are being helped by the Polish guards to escape.'

When it came to his own escape, the daredevil Skorzeny did it in style. Three former SS officers dressed in the uniforms of the

United States Military Police turned up and told the guard that they had come to collect the prisoner Skorzeny for the next day's hearing at Nuremberg.

Funding the operation

In the last days of the war Skorzeny withdrew to the 'Alpine redoubt' in Bavaria, an underground fortress where a group of Nazi fanatics intended to make their last stand. Art treasures and munitions factories had been moved to the caves to protect them from bombing. Adolf Eichmann also turned up. He had with him 22 crates filled with valuables stolen from his Jewish victims in the extermination camps, which included gold teeth and wedding rings. The Vienna State Prosecutor's Office estimated that 'Eichmann's gold' was worth $8 million in 1955. Key documents were also said to have been taken there. The prisoners who had been forging British bank notes in Sachsenhausen concentration camp were transferred to Mauthausen-Gusen concentration camp, near Linz in Austria. Adolf Burger, whose wife and parents had been killed in the death camps, recalled that they also forged Argentinian and other travel documents:

We printed Brazilian passports, Tunisian identity cards, British and American military passes and shipmasters' certificates. We even produced metal dies. Once we forged Dutch baptismal certificates, then there were official deeds from French cities or letterheads from the Palestine office in Geneva, with wording in Hebrew script. We forged British marriage certificates and a US army paybook.

Everything you would need, in fact, if you wanted to change your identity.

A witness once saw Nazis sinking crates in Lake Toplitz. Divers found one of the containers in 1959. When they prised the lid open with a crowbar, British £5 notes floated to the surface. Diving there is now banned. Most of the money found its way into the hands of a shady character called Friedrich Schwend, alias Wendig, who was arrested at the end of the war but soon released. After he had been issued with a Yugoslav passport bearing the name 'Wenceslav Turi', the CIC allowed him to leave Germany with his wife. He settled in Lima, Peru where he became 'head of ODESSA in South America', according to an informant.

Other funds were available to ODESSA, in Schwend's absence. When it became certain that Germany was faced with defeat, a number of wealthy Germans moved their money out of the country. By 1946, it was estimated that assets worth two billion Swiss francs were on deposit in Switzerland.

Escape routes

Skorzeny's ODESSA role was discovered when an American agent infiltrated a Nazi network known as the 'Brotherhood'. The former *Waffen-SS* colonel was also thought to have run an operation called 'The Spider', which ran an escape route into Italy. Fugitives were transported in the German-driven trucks that delivered the American army newspaper *Stars and Stripes*.

The Catholic Church played a major role in the organization. In Rome, Austrian Bishop Alois Hudal assisted former SS men by finding accommodation, providing travel documents and making arrangements to get them out of the country. In 1937, Hudal published *The Foundations of National Socialism*, a book that praised Hitler. He sent a copy to the *Führer*, calling him 'the new Siegfried of Germany's greatness'. The bishop was helped by a former Nazi counter-intelligence officer named Reinhard Kops, who sifted through the details of the new refugees arriving in Rome. Other Catholic clerics helped. It is not known if Pope Pius XII was involved, but Cardinal Giovanni Battista Montini (later Pope Paul VI) certainly lent a hand.

Many people lost their travel documents during the war, but it was easy to obtain a passport from the International Committee of the Red Cross on the recommendation of a priest. The archbishop of Genoa, Giuseppe Siri, set up a committee to help refugees get to Argentina. He put them in touch with the Argentine Immigration Commission in Europe, which was run by Franz Ruffinengo, a former officer in Mussolini's army. Juan Perón, who had become president of Argentina in 1946, wanted to turn the country into a military and industrial power along the lines of Nazi Germany and Fascist Italy, so he was keen to recruit 'technicians'. Meanwhile he established the anti-Semitic 'National Ethnic Institute'.

Perón wanted to turn Argentina into a military power along the lines of Nazi Germany, so he was keen to recruit 'technicians'

Perón's immigration policy in Buenos Aires was handled by Rodolfo Freude and Horst Carlos Fuldner. Freude was a blond-haired Argentinian whose German father had close ties with the Nazis during the war and Fuldner was a German–Argentinian former SS captain who had served in the SD. In March 1945, Fuldner had travelled to Madrid to set up an escape route for other SS men. When the Allies had demanded his extradition in 1947 he had fled to Argentina, a place where former SS men were granted immunity. Adolf Eichmann, Josef Mengele, Erich Priebke, Josef Schwammberger and Gerhard Bohne escaped this way.

Erich Priebke would have lived out his days as a free man if his arrogant nature had not led him to share his shameful past with a television audience. At the end of the war, Priebke was captured by the British, but he managed to escape. He was then hidden by a family in Sterzing, on the Austrian border. Eichmann and Mengele had also taken refuge there. In 1948, Bishop Hudal made arrangements for him to leave the country, so he fled to Argentina.

He had been living in Argentina for 50 years when he unwisely gave a television interview in which he admitted his part in the deportation of over 11,000 Italian Jews to Auschwitz. He said he had only been following the orders of SS Lieutenant-Colonel Herbert Kappler, the chief of the Gestapo in Rome. Kappler had been sentenced to life imprisonment by an Italian military tribunal, but his wife had smuggled him out of jail in a large suitcase in 1977, when he had been suffering from terminal cancer. He died in Germany in the following year.

Priebke's television revelations were only the tip of the iceberg, though. On another occasion he had shot 335 Italian civilians at the Ardeatine caves in Rome, while he was a captain in the *Waffen-SS*. He was exacting a reprisal for the shooting of 33 SS military policemen, who had been killed by Italian partisans on 23 March 1944.

The outrage over Priebke's TV interview led to him being extradited to Italy to face trial. SS Lieutenant-Colonel Karl Hass, a former SD man who had assisted Priebke in the massacre, was going to be the chief witness. Hass was hiding out in an Italian monastery when he was recruited by the CIC. He agreed to return to Italy so that he could testify against Priebke in return for immunity, but he changed his mind at the last minute. While attempting to escape from his hotel room by climbing down from the balcony, he slipped and fell. Still a captive, he was now injured as well, so he had to testify from his hospital bed. Hass was deemed to have broken the agreement that had given him immunity, so he was held under house arrest until his death in 2004. His testimony led to the conviction of Priebke, who was sentenced to life imprisonment under house arrest.

Josef Schwammberger was another SS war criminal who managed to escape to Argentina. During the Second World War, he was the sadistic commander of a number of SS forced labour camps around Krakow in Poland. Captured in the French occupation zone in 1945, he was sent by rail to the United States military authorities in Austria, where he was going to stand trial. However, he made his escape from a moving train. Although he travelled to Argentina on an Italian passport, he lived there under his own name, becoming an Argentinian citizen in 1965.

In 1973, the German authorities informed the Argentinian government that Schwammberger was on their top ten list of wanted Nazis, but it took until 1987 to locate him. He was extradited in 1989 and was eventually convicted of seven counts of murder and 32 counts of accessory to murder. Denied parole because of the unusual cruelty of his offences, he died in jail.

Gerhard Bohne also found the air in Argentina more congenial at one point. How much of a war criminal he had been is a matter for conjecture, but he had certainly been part of the T-4 Euthanasia Programme. The legally trained Bohne, then an SS first lieutenant, resigned his position in 1942 after accusing his colleagues of misusing motor vehicles as well as 'alcoholic and sexual excesses'. Captured by the Americans in Italy, he was released in 1946. He then returned to Germany, where he worked as a legal assistant.

In 1949, he fled to Argentina where he wrote for *Der Weg* (The Way), a German-language National Socialist journal that was published in the Perón era. After returning to Germany in 1956 he was admitted to the Bar in Düsseldorf, but in 1959 he was charged with complicity in the murder of at least 15,000 people. Bailed for health reasons, he escaped to Denmark and then travelled to Buenos Aires via Zurich. He was arrested in Argentina in 1964 and extradited to Germany two years later. However, the legal procedures dragged on until he had a heart attack in 1968. All charges against him were dropped in the following year.

Working for the West

The CIC was also using the Catholic Church's 'ratlines' (systems of escape routes) to smuggle American agents and informants out of Europe. The most notorious case was that of the 'butcher of Lyon', Klaus Barbie. A former SS captain, Barbie was on both the French and the American wanted lists when he cut a deal with the CIC.

'We simply knew very little about the

SAMEDI 4/07/1987

CLC / Ville de Lyon

Klaus Barbie, 'the butcher of Lyon', escaped to Bolivia after the war and lived there for 30 years under the name of Klaus Altmann

Russians, about their army, their tactics, battle-plans and so forth,' said Jim Milano who used the ratlines, 'and there was a good deal of pressure on the secret service to get hold of this information.'

Himmler had fought tooth and nail to make the SS a communist-free zone. As a result, several Western organizations eagerly recruited former SS men in their war against Soviet espionage. When Barbie approached the CIC, they did not arrest him but instead used his skills by employing him as an interrogator. He was also ordered to infiltrate the Communist Party in Bavaria.

'In view of the great value he was to our organization, we had no great pangs of conscience,' said one of his American colleagues.

When the French demanded Barbie's extradition, the CIC simply arranged for him to flee to Latin America, where he worked closely with Friedrich Schwend and became an adviser to the Bolivian secret service. It is thought that Gestapo chief Heinrich Müller and Eichmann's 'best man' Alois Brunner disappeared in a similar fashion. Some former SS men even went to live in the United States or Canada. Both countries were happy to take communist-hating immigrants on board, even if they had been members of the SS.

Thanks to the Cold War, Barbie remained a free man for many years. He had not always been the 'butcher of Lyon', however. As a young man he had intended to study theology, but he gave up his further education plans when his father died. He was then conscripted into the Reich Labour Service (RAD), an organization that had been formed to reduce unemployment. In 1935, he joined the SD. After serving in the German-occupied Netherlands he was posted to Lyon, where he headed the local Gestapo.

From his headquarters in the Hotel Terminus, he oversaw the torture and death of over 4,000 people. He then condemned a further 7,500 innocent citizens to the death camps, including numerous children. Barbie personally tortured his victims in the most barbarous fashion. He burned them, beat them, half-drowned them, administered electric shocks to their nipples or genitals and pushed needles under their fingernails. On top of all that, he staged mock executions.

'It really amused him to see others suffer,' said one victim.

His most famous victim was Jean Moulin, head of the French Resistance, who died from the treatment he received at Barbie's hands.

In 1945, Barbie was being pursued by MI5. Instead of running, he approached MI6, who gladly recruited the former mass murderer. However, some people found it impossible to overlook his heinous crimes. While he was in Hamburg he was beaten up by British soldiers and locked in a coal cellar for three days. His experience caused him to develop a grudge against the British, so he turned to the CIC, who welcomed him with open arms. He used his position to help other SS men escape. When the French learnt that he was in the American zone, they wanted him back, so in 1951 he was spirited off to Bolivia. Twenty years later he was tracked down by Nazi hunters, but it was not until 1983 that he was extradited to France. At his trial, he refused to defend himself. He was sentenced to life imprisonment and he died in jail.

Alois Brunner was another big fish that got

> **Barbie personally tortured his victims, burning them, beating them and pushing needles under their fingernails**

away. Brunner was responsible for sending at least 120,000 people to their deaths. He had been in charge of seizing and deporting Jews in Austria, Slovakia, France and Greece. In 1945, he kept out of the Allies' hands by the simple expedient of changing his name to Alois Schmaldienst. Although he was eventually detained by both the British and the Americans, he was soon released. He even went to work as a driver for the United States occupation forces.

When things got too hot for him in Germany, he escaped to Syria via Rome and Cairo. Former Nazis were welcomed there, especially after the foundation of Israel in 1948. First of all he worked as an arms dealer and then he was taken on by the Syrian secret service. However, Mossad, the Israeli intelligence agency, eventually discovered where he was. Israelis were not exactly welcome in Syria, so they let the postman do the job of getting to Brunner. He lost his left eye when a letter bomb exploded in 1961. A parcel bomb blew off both of his hands in 1980.

Brunner has been sentenced to death twice in absentia. Rumours of his death have not been confirmed.

Well looked after

When SS men escaped at the end of the war, they were often well looked after. Money was smuggled out to them through the office Skorzeny had set up in Madrid and German manufacturers with factories in other parts of the world were asked to employ fleeing Nazis. Adolf Eichmann worked in the Volkswagen plant in Argentina, for example.

Some former SS members even went on to live a comfortable life at the expense of the British and American governments, provided they had some technical or scientific expertise to offer. The most famous of these was Wernher von Braun, the chief architect of the Saturn V launch vehicle and the rocket boosters that carried Apollo 11 to the moon. As an SS major, he had developed the V-2 ballistic missiles that had devastated London and Antwerp. These weapons had been built in an underground factory in Dora-Mittelbau, where thousands of slave labourers had been worked to death. It was not until 1979, two years after von Braun's death, that the United States Department of Justice set up the Office of Special Investigations. Its purpose was to apprehend all those who had committed crimes against humanity. Former Nazis were a prime target. It seems that former SS members could escape justice in numerous ways without the help of ODESSA. A number of other organizations also provided them with material assistance. One of them was the Comrades' Welfare Society founded by Hans-Ulrich Rudel, a *Luftwaffe* air ace who had escaped to Argentina with the aid of the Catholic Church. Rudel's organization helped with legal costs and it also sent parcels of food

Former SS man Wernher von Braun, seen here with his arm in plaster, brought his knowledge of rockets to the US space programme

and clothing. Among those who received these care packages were the families of Rudolf Hess and Admiral Dönitz. Rudel acted as an agent for the agricultural machinery that was built by Josef Mengele's family firm in Bavaria and he also maintained close ties with Juan Perón. His closest associate, Willem Sassen, a Dutch SS member, worked closely with Augusto Pinochet, the president of Chile, and Alfredo Stroessner, the president of Paraguay. Life could be good in Argentina. Raucous groups of unrepentant SS veterans held 'brownshirt parties' and toasted the 'good old days'.

In 1951, an organization called *Stille Hilfe*

Former air ace Hans-Ulrich Rudel founded the Comrades' Welfare Society after escaping to Argentina with the help of the Catholic Church

(Silent Aid) was set up to provide assistance to convicted Nazi war criminals. High-ranking former SS officers sat on its board, along with prominent members of the Church. Its first president was Princess Helene Elisabeth von Isenburg, also known as the 'Mother of the Landsbergers'. The Landsbergers were the Nazis who still languished in Landsberg Prison. A leading member of the operation was Gudrun Burwitz, *née* Himmler – the *Reichsführer's* beloved daughter, whom he had referred to as 'Püppi'.

At around the same time, the Mutual Aid Association for Soldiers of the Former *Waffen-SS* (HIAG) was set up. For years it was run by SS General Kurt Meyer

One of his aims was to rehabilitate the reputation of the *Waffen-SS*. He maintained that its members were merely soldiers and had nothing to do with the crimes of the *Allgemeine-SS*. The organization's spokesman was Hans Wissebach, a member of the German parliament, or Bundestag, and a former member of the *Leibstandarte SS Adolf Hitler*. As well as

the HIAG main office, there were hundreds of local and regional groups where former SS men could get together and reminisce. The HIAG was dissolved in 1992, but its journal *Der Freiwillige* (The Volunteer) continued to be published. Its youth group – *Wiking-Jugend* (Viking Youth) – was banned in 1994.

All of the former members of the SS are now dead, or too frail to do any harm. However, the seeds that spawned the SS are still there. In 1979 the Aid Organization for National Political Prisoners (HNG) was set up along the lines of *Stille Hilfe*. Its aim was to help neo-Nazis 'who have, out of political conviction, committed acts of arson against accommodation of asylum seekers, inflicted bodily harm or been guilty of other criminal behaviour'.

The banned *Wiking-Jugend* has been replaced by the Friends of Ulrich von Hutten, a 16th-century poet and patriot who is romanticized in German literature as a freedom fighter. Its journal *Huttenbriefe* (Hutten Letters) calls for the establishment of a 'Fourth Reich', where there would be a need for a new SS.